MW01054231

Hot Haute Cuisine

Recipes to Excite

Philippa Sklaar

Edited by Penny Hozy

NDE Publishing 2003

Hot Cuisine: Recipes to Excite

By Philippa Sklaar

Edited by Penny Hozy
Design: Multistudio Advertising Inc.
Photography: Gregory Talas
Cover photo: Trinette Reed/Getty Images © 2003

© 2003 by Philippa Sklaar

© 2003 by NDE Publishing ™

Printed in Singapore

All rights reserved. No part of this publication may be reproduced, stored in a retrieval system or transmitted in any form or by any means, electronic, mechanical, photocopied, recorded or otherwise, without written permission from:

Elena Mazour, Publisher
NDE Publishing
15-30 Wertheim Court
Richmond Hill, ON L4B 1B9
tel: 905-731-1288
toll free: 800-675-1263
fax: 905-731-5744
e-mail: info@ndepublishing.com
url: www.ndepublishing.com

National Library of Canada Cataloguing in Publication:

Sklaar, Philippa, 1960-
    Hot cuisine : recipes to excite / Philippa Sklaar ; edited by Penny Hozy.

ISBN 1-55321-100-6

    1. Cookery. I. Hozy, Penny, 1947- II. Title.

TX714.S454 2003   641.5   C2003-902407-5

DISCLAIMER
The recipes in this book have been carefully tested by our kitchen and our tasters. To the best of our knowledge, they are safe and nutritious for ordinary use and users. For those people with food or other allergies, who have special food requirements or health issues, please read the suggested ingredients and method for each recipe carefully to determine whether or not they may create a problem for you. All such recipes are used at the risk of the consumer.
We cannot be responsible for any hazards, loss or damage which may occur as a result of any such recipe use.
For those with special needs or requirements, allergies, or health problems, in the event of any doubt, please contact your medical advisor prior to the use of any such recipe.

NDE Publishing is a trademark of NDE Canada Corp.

When my son Mathew was 11, he put a recipe of his own on my computer.

1 teaspoon Mathew

1 teaspoon Jamie

1 tablespoon Tabasco

1 dessert spoon Philippa (must be seasoned with guilt)

1 cup of understanding

and a teaspoon of patience (a litre if Philippa is used)

Mix all ingredients together and heat at 200 degrees Celsius.
(If Philippa is in one of her moods heat at 5 degrees Celsius.)
Serve hot.

Table of Contents

Chapter One:
Fatal Attractions

Starters

Think foreplay – tantalizing, teasing, seductive, and delicious with the promise of more to come.

Chapter Two:
Love Potions

Soups

I was astonished at the success my soups have with men. If I had known that all it would take is one of these soups, I would have spent a lot less on lingerie and lipstick.

Chapter Three:
Sensuous Discoveries

Salads

For me, Sundays in summer mean a table laden with wonderful, brightly coloured salads, and watching my muscled lover standing over the barbecue in the hot sun, imagining what I am going to do to him once the guests have left.

Vegetables

The most frequent requests from women who attend my cooking classes are for interesting & delicious vegetable dishes to impress their men. Of course I can oblige! A good vegetable accompaniment elevates a meal to another dimension.

Chapter Four:

See me, Feel me, Touch me, Tempt me

Pasta

What woman doesn't dream about sitting opposite a tall, dark & gorgeous man, with candlelight flickering, sipping wine and twirling pasta in a rich sauce into her mouth and being told by his eyes that she is more delectable than the food?

Pizza

All the best words start with P. Pizza, Passion, Pamper, Perfect!

Chapter Five:

Reeling Them In

Seafood

If you want a man to fall for you – hook, line and sinker – nothing will impress him more than a sensational fish dish.

Chapter Six:

Birds of a Feather Sleep Together

Poultry

I see the main course as "The Relationship." The neurotic part is over, no more obsessing over a ringing telephone, and I can catch my breath after the chase. What can compare to the luxurious feeling of having a pair of gorgeous arms to sink into at the end of each day?

Chapter Seven:

Put Fire in His Loins

Beef, Lamb and Veal

Even though these days red meat is considered by some to be unhealthy, there is nothing like a marvelous meat dish to overwhelm your man completely. If you are looking for total conquest, any of the following recipes will enslave him.

Chapter Eight:
Make the Love Rise

Breads

There isn't a man on earth who isn't impressed with a woman who makes her own bread. Accept that he will be around for life, because once he has sunk his teeth into any of these breads you will never be able to get rid of him!

Sandwiches

Every boyfriend (and husband) I have had gets euphoric when they talk about the sandwiches I make. Forget about sexy lingerie, dim lights & scented oils – these sandwiches hit the spot quicker and more effectively than any words whispered in his ear.

Chapter Nine:

Cookies

The ultimate sophisticated seduction is serving tea in a silver tea set with an assortment of any of these cookies – presented on a silver platter, of course. Or they're just fabulous to stuff into your mouth after a bout of wild, passionate bedroom gymnastics!

Chapter Ten:

Breakfast Bliss, Muffins & Sweet Buns

For me muffins and breakfast dishes have always conjured up thoughts of Sunday mornings with a delicious lover, the sheets all tangled, the newspapers scattered on the floor & eating naked in bed.

Chapter Eleven:

Ultimate Temptations

Desserts And Cakes

For some reason men look at desserts the same sensuous way they look at an attractive woman. So, if you wish to cultivate this look in your man, any of these desserts is guaranteed to do the trick.

Haute Cuisine

Recipes to Excite

Introduction

My love affair with food started when I was on honeymoon with my first husband, "Tabasco." I had been brought up in a home where the smells of cooking & baking permeated the air from dawn to dusk. My grandmother, an exceptional cook who never followed a recipe, prepared all the meals in our home. Whenever my mother asked her how much of an ingredient she put into a dish, she would pinch her fingers together to indicate the quantity. If pressed to give the exact amount, she became outraged and would reply in her heavy Yiddish accent, "I'm dead? Dhere's someting wrong mit me? You tink I can't make it?" And off she would waddle into the kitchen.

My grandmother passed this cooking gene onto my mother, who is also a fantastic cook. It was from my grandmother that I inherited the talent for being able to cook something just from having tasted it. It is from both of them that I inherited a passion for cooking. They also passed on to me their tendency to have affairs, (not the culinary kind) but then that's another meal altogether.

Food & romance have been in my family for generations. My grandmother met my grandfather in a restaurant in Kelm in Lithuania. She was having a meal with her sister when in walked a tall, dark and gorgeous man. She couldn't take her eyes off him. Not wanting to waste any time she scribbled a note on a napkin and called the waiter over to give it to him. She had written, "I like compliments." He looked up from reading it and smiled. They were married six months later.

A few years later they moved to South Africa where my grandmother ran a successful dressmaking business. At one point she fell in love with her bookkeeper and had an affair with him. Years later when her health was failing, my mother took her out for a drive to try and cheer her up. My grandmother did not show the slightest interest in where they were going until my mother said she was taking her to meet her latest lover. My grandmother perked up and replied, "Vell, every voman must have an interest in life." With these women forming my gene pool, is it any wonder I turned out the same way?

Cooking and male conquests have run side by side in my life and every time I would bring home a new "this is the one," my mother would roll her eyes and say, "Another one who will give you trips, trinkets and tears." And of course she was always right, but at least I got to go on the most marvelous trips all over the world where I was able to satisfy my insatiable need to learn about cooking. If only I had been as quick to learn about men as I was about food!

One of the lessons my mother taught me was that the table should be set beautifully every evening. Any condiments had to be decanted into exquisite containers before being put out. We never had any food that was packaged or pre-cooked – that included anything frozen or tinned as well as fast food.

So it was that I found myself on honeymoon at the age of twenty, overwhelmed on waking up the morning after to discover that lunchtime was approaching and I had no idea what to do, what to make or how to make it. Because of my upbringing, it didn't even occur to me that I could just buy something ready made or order take-out. The simplest meal I could think of was a salad, but not knowing how to make mayonnaise, I rang my mother for instructions. My journey into men and food had begun.

When I look back at the relationships I have had over the years, the one thing that I always had in common with my men was food. There is no doubt that I have proved the old cliché that the way to a man's heart is through his stomach. I have remained friendly with all my ex's, mainly because they love my cooking and go starry-eyed when they recall the meals I prepared for them. I have little patience, (instant gratification is something I understand very well) so my style of cooking is quick, easy, glamorous and

…men speak only one language coherently, and that's the language of food.

delicious. I am an aesthetic junkie and love combining colors, textures and tastes. I see the world through food so I have dishes that suit my every mood – comfort food, indulgent food, nostalgic food, romantic food, bringing-up-children food, mending-broken-heart food, seduction food and food for when I am just plain hungry.

Like my mother, I regard serving a meal as a production – from the table linen to the candles, to the flowers, to the presentation of the food. All the senses should be seduced and titillated. I am often reminded of that wonderful expression that God is in the details. Remember that when preparing the scene for seduction.

As my romances came and went, the only steady passion in my life was cooking. I hope you will enjoy these recipes as much as I have enjoyed creating them, serving them and eating them. Acquiring these recipes has been a long journey and an education – not only about food but also about men, relationships and often about growing up. So, if it's a man you're after, forget the theory that men come from Mars. My experience is that men speak only one language coherently, and that's the language of food.

Cast of Charachters

First boyfriend
Oyster
– the food always associated with passion.
He introduced me to the world of sensuous discoveries.

First husband
Tabasco
– fiery, moody, raging, needs to be tempered
– usually with a good dose of love!

Second husband
Icicle
– looks great on the outside, but it's just an icy mask covering a hard and cold center.

Another boyfriend
Hamburger
– his favorite food – nothing hits the spot better than a great hamburger.
And then it always feels like it disappears far too soon. Just like he did.

And another boyfriend
Caviar
– Oh so indulgent and sooo satisfying.

An interlude
Butterscotch
– tempting, delicious and best appreciated in small quantities.

And one more boyfriend
Better Than Chocolate
– easily compared to a smorgasbord of sensory overload.

Chapter One

Fatal Attractions

Starters

**Think foreplay – tantalizing, teasing, seductive,
and delicious with the promise of more to come.**

Sky's The Limit Crêpes

I met my first husband, "Tabasco," on the island of Mauritius. When we were chosen to represent our team in the breast painting competition, our fate was sealed! I was lying on my back with my top off, my legs dangling on either side of a bench, while he stood astride, leaning over me with a paintbrush in his hand, dipping it into pots of paint and coloring my nipples.

Later that day we ate these crêpes. They will forever remind me of light feathery strokes caressing my flesh.

This recipe is as good now as it was then. It can be served as a starter, as a light lunch with a salad and homemade bread, or as part of a buffet.

Crêpes

It is best to use a crêpe maker but if not available, use a non-stick frying pan.

> 1 1/2 cups milk
> 1 tablespoon cooking oil
> 3 eggs
> 1 1/2 cups flour
> pinch salt
> 1/2 tsp oregano

Place all the ingredients in a food processor. Blend until smooth. If too thick add a little milk and if too runny add a little flour. If using a non-stick pan, spray the pan very lightly with a pan coating spray. Pour in enough batter to cover the bottom of the pan with a thin layer. Cook the first side until it is brown and flip to cook the other side. Separate each cooked crêpe with plastic wrap. They can be made in advance, and kept either in the fridge or freezer.

Fillings

Use any filling ingredients, but these are my favorites:

> 2 smoked trout
> 2 peppered mackerel
> 8oz/250g smoked salmon (optional)
> 2 x 8oz/250ml tubs cream cheese
>   seasoned with salt, black pepper,
>   cayenne pepper and paprika
> 2 avocados, mashed and seasoned with salt,
>   black pepper and lemon juice,
>   or guacamole
> ½ cup Homemade Mayonnaise
>   (recipe page 41) mixed with
>   1–2 teaspoons beet horseradish

To serve, place one crêpe on a cake platter or round serving dish. Spread with one of the fillings and then place another crêpe on top. Continue to make layers of different fillings, each separated by a crêpe, until all the fillings are used up. Place in the fridge for a few hours to set. Sprinkle with paprika and garnish with parsley, watercress or chives. Surround with salad greens and serve.

I was lying on my back with my top off, my legs dangling on either side of a bench, while he stood astride…

Wanton Chinese Wontons

1 cup boneless chicken breasts

4 scallions

1 tablespoon soy sauce

1 tablespoon oyster sauce

2 teaspoons sugar

1 teaspoon five-spice powder

½ teaspoon ginger

½ cup water chestnuts, chopped

1 package Chinese spring roll wrappers

1 cup grated carrots

egg white, unbeaten

oil for deep frying – enough to cover wontons

Place the chicken, scallions and all the seasonings in a food processor and process until smooth. Fold in water chestnuts. Lay the spring roll pastry on a work surface and cut into 4 equal parts to measure 2"/5cm. Place a little grated carrot in the center of each square and top with a teaspoon of chicken mixture. Brush all around the edges with egg white (not beaten) and lift the sides up to meet above the filling to form a wonton. Press the edges together firmly. Deep fry until golden brown and drain on paper towels.

Thai Dipping Sauce

1 cup white vinegar

½ cup water

½ cup sugar

¼ cup brown sugar

1–2 dried chilies

1 tablespoon soy sauce

2 teaspoons cornstarch mixed to a paste with cold water

1 teaspoon salt

minced garlic to taste

1 teaspoon chopped cilantro

1 cup cucumber, thinly sliced

Heat all the ingredients except the cilantro and cucumber until the sugar dissolves. Add the cucumber and cilantro and serve at room temperature.

I read an article in the newspaper about the Oriental Hotel in Bangkok having a cooking school & persuaded my sister, Louise, to go with me. I had never been to the Far East and could not contain my excitement knowing that I was going to one of the best hotels in the world to do what I love best. I was seeing Hamburger at the time and he generously agreed to indulge this whim of mine. All the recipes in this book that have a Thai influence are from that trip.

Playful Pot

Yields approximately 24

I love these and they are a wow every time I serve them. They are especially yummy when you pop them into his mouth and he licks your fingers clean.

6 boneless chicken breasts
1 teaspoon ginger
1 teaspoon sugar
1 tablespoon soy sauce
1 tablespoon oyster sauce
black pepper to taste
3 scallions
1 package pot sticker wrappers or spring roll wrappers cut into 3"/5cm circles
oil for cooking

Place chicken, spices and scallions in food processor and process until well mixed. Brush edges of pastry with water and place a teaspoon of chicken filling in the center of each square. Bring the edges together above the filling and stick together to form little parcels. These may be frozen at this stage – cover with plastic wrap.

Sauce

¼ cup lemon juice
1 teaspoon grated lemon peel
3 tablespoons sugar
2 tablespoons sherry
1 tablespoon soy sauce
2 teaspoons chili paste
1 tablespoon minced ginger
salt to taste

Combine all the above ingredients and set aside.

Heat 4-5 tablespoons oil in a pan. Place pot stickers upright in the oil and cook for a few minutes until the bottoms are lightly browned. Add sauce and cover with a lid. Reduce heat and steam for a few minutes until wontons are firm to the touch. Remove the lid and continue to cook until the sauce reduces. Make sure that the sauce glazes over each wonton evenly. Serve immediately.

Stickers

Sexy Samosas

Any combination of ingredients may be used for the filling – vegetables, leftover chicken, beef or lamb seasoned with curry and mixed together with peas and cubed potatoes make these sensational.

1 large onion, chopped

1 cup grated cheddar cheese

salt and pepper to taste

1 package spring roll wrappers

Chinese sweet chili sauce or chutney for dipping

oil for deep frying

Samosas have serious sentimental value for me. It was after a dozen samosas and a bottle of red wine that I lost my virginity to Oyster. After all these years I still can't take a bite out of a samosa without a warm blush coming to my face.

Cook onions till glossy in 3 tablespoons of oil. In a bowl, mix the onions with the cheddar cheese and season with salt and pepper. Allow mixture to cool. Place one sheet of spring roll pastry on a work surface. Lightly wet the edges of the pastry with some water. Spoon a tablespoon of cheese and onion onto the top right hand corner of the pastry. Fold the pastry over the mixture in the same way as folding a flag, to form a triangle. Finish the rest of the mixture, using one spring roll wrapper per samosa. Heat about an inch of oil in a frying pan. Cook both sides of the samosas till golden brown. Drain on paper towels and serve with either chutney or Chinese sweet chili sauce for dipping.

The Promise of Potato Straws with

Cooking with Better Than Chocolate is an incomparable treat. He made this for me one night with a lot of sipping of wine, kissing, chopping, stirring, more kissing, and tasting. Having him in the kitchen is my idea of heaven and this dish comes straight from there.

These never fail to get sounds of appreciation whenever I serve them. They also work well made in a miniature version and served with drinks.

> 4 potatoes, washed and grated
>   (I often don't peel them)
> oil for deep frying
> smoked salmon
>   (smoked salmon trout may also be used)
> crème fraîche (½ cup heavy cream
>   mixed with ½ cup sour cream)
> parsley, lemon wedges & chives for garnishing

Drain grated potatoes in a salad spinner to ensure that all the water drains from them. Heat oil in non-stick frying pan. Place enough of the grated potato into the oil to form a circle the size of a saucer. Flatten with a spatula. Cook till golden brown, turn over and cook other side. Drain on paper towels. These may be cooked well in advance and if they get soft, crisp them up in the oven.

Place on individual plates, and top with a generous amount of smoked salmon and a dollop of the crème fraîche. Sprinkle with freshly ground black pepper and garnish with lemon wedges, parsley or chives. Surround with salad greens, drizzle with a Vinaigrette Dressing (recipes page 40) and serve. If serving with drinks, each potato straw should measure about 2"/4–5cm in diameter.

Smoked Salmon & Crème Fraîche

Tuna Tartare Temptation

Better Than Chocolate made this one evening and I am convinced he cast a spell over me. As my taste buds met with his tuna tartare, my eyes glazed over, my pulses raced, and my head exploded with my very first gastronomic orgasm. I often have euphoric flashbacks whenever I think of this dish, as well as what happened afterwards…

Serves 6

2lb/1kg sushi-grade tuna,
   chopped into small cubes

1 small sweet onion, finely chopped

½ tablespoon fresh minced ginger

¼ cup chopped cilantro

½ teaspoon finely minced garlic

1 tablespoon sesame oil

juice of ½ lemon

2 tablespoons sesame seeds

1 teaspoon chili paste
   mixed with 3 tablespoons mayonnaise

pinch sugar

salt

¼ cup smelt eggs

Place all the above ingredients, except the smelt eggs, in a mixing bowl. Adjust seasonings. Gently fold in the smelt eggs. Place in a mold and invert onto individual plates.

Cilantro Sauce

1 cup cilantro

1–2 tablespoons honey

½ teaspoon minced garlic

½ teaspoon minced fresh ginger

2–3 tablespoons rice wine vinegar

splash of lemon juice

salt and pepper to taste

½ cup olive oil

Place all the ingredients, except the oil, in a food processor. Mix well. While the motor is running, slowly pour the olive oil in until the sauce emulsifies. Adjust seasonings and pour into a squeeze bottle. Set aside. Freeze or refrigerate leftover sauce.

French Bread Toast

1 loaf French bread
olive oil
1 lemon
minced garlic
finely chopped cilantro

Preheat oven to 350F/180C degrees. Slice the French bread thinly and on the diagonal. Place slices on a baking sheet. Drizzle with olive oil and splash with lemon juice on both sides. Rub the cilantro and garlic over one side and place in the oven till lightly browned. Set aside.

To Serve

lemon-infused olive oil
crème fraîche
caviar
chives

Gently squeeze the cilantro sauce around the tuna tartare. Drizzle some lemon-infused olive oil next to it. Spoon a dollop of crème fraîche on top of the tuna tartare and top it off with a teaspoon of caviar. Place 2 chives in each mound to garnish. Place 2 slices French Bread Toast on each plate.

Sinful Potato Skins

I often serve these as a starter or a light lunch dish with a salad. They light up a man's eyes better than a sexy centerfold!

6–8 potatoes

cooking oil for brushing potatoes

bunch of scallions, chopped

1 cup cheddar cheese, grated

flaked smoked chicken marinated in barbecue sauce (optional)

parsley or cilantro for garnishing

Bake or microwave potatoes until soft. Allow to cool. Cut in half, scoop out the insides and discard, being careful not to break the skin and leaving a thin layer of potato all the way around the inside. Place on a greased baking sheet skin-side up. Brush with oil and bake in a 350F/180C oven until crisp. Turn potatoes over and fill with a dollop of sour cream. Sprinkle some scallions and grated cheese on top. Place under broiler or bake until bubbling.

If using smoked chicken, allow to marinate in barbecue sauce for 30 minutes. After the potato skins have been crisped in the oven, fill them with the chicken and serve with chopped parsley, scallions or cilantro.

Chapter Two

Love Potions

I was astonished at the success my soups have with men. If I had known that
all it would take is one of these soups, I would have spent a lot less
on lingerie & lipstick.

Exotic Oriental Soup

I always thought it would be romantic to ride on an elephant in the jungle. So I convinced one of my men to take me to Thailand. I loved it, he hated it – the elephant's skin felt like pot scourers – but I got the idea for this soup on that trip.

We often saw people in the markets eating bowls of soup filled with the most marvelous combination of ingredients. It's a meal in a bowl and quite a showstopper. Shellfish may be used instead of chicken or beef.

Chicken Stock

1 chicken

3–4 carrots

3–4 parsnips (for which I have a passion)

4 leeks

3–4 tablespoons powdered chicken stock

1 tablespoon minced fresh ginger

2 tablespoons chopped parsley

salt and pepper to taste

2 eggs, beaten

Place chicken with carrots, parsnips and leeks in a large pot filled with water. Bring to the boil and then simmer for 2 hours. Strain, cool and skim fat off the soup. Season with 3–4 tablespoons powdered chicken stock, fresh ginger, parsley, salt and pepper to taste. When stock is boiling, slowly drizzle in 2 beaten eggs between the tines of a fork. Stir the soup well, making sure the egg is distributed evenly. Adjust seasonings and keep warm.

Accompaniment for Soup

1 package spring roll wrappers

oil for deep frying

green beans for garnishing

2 cups beef (fillet or sirloin)
  or 4 boneless chicken breasts, thinly sliced and marinated in 2 tablespoons soy sauce, a little garlic and juice of ½ lemon

6 leaves of Chinese cabbage

Cut spring roll wrappers into 1"/2cm squares (enough to fill 2 cups) and deep fry in hot oil till golden brown and crispy. Drain on paper towels and set aside. Steam green beans and twist into a pretzel shape and set those aside. (The steaming makes them pliable enough not to snap.) Cook beef or chicken in 2 tablespoons oil until done. Slice each leaf of the Chinese cabbage down the center.

To Serve

toasted sesame seeds

2–3 tablespoons freshly chopped cilantro
 or parsley

1 cup bean sprouts

1 bunch scallions, finely chopped

1 package egg noodles cooked,
 rinsed and set aside (one-minute noodles
 are great – use 2 packages)

Ladle soup into bowls over a piece of Chinese cabbage.
Heat the steak/chicken and place in the soup along with
the sesame seeds, cilantro, bean sprouts, scallions, heated
noodles, and spring roll squares. Garnish with pretzel-
shaped string beans and cilantro leaves.

This is my all-time favorite soup to serve in summer. It's absolutely fat-free, looks great and is always a winner. I served it as a starter at my second wedding. In a contest between the soup and the groom, the soup won hands down!

ngaging Gazpacho

1 onion

2 English cucumbers, unpeeled

4 large tomatoes

1 cup cooked and puréed butternut squash

2 cups tomato juice

1 cup ice water

2 teaspoons cumin

1 teaspoon salt

black pepper to taste

few drops Tabasco

pinch of cayenne pepper

1 tablespoon brown sugar

3 tablespoons brown or malt vinega

Topping :

2 avocados, peeled, pitted and chopped

plain yogurt

chives or watercress for garnish

Grate the onion, cucumber and tomatoes. Place in a bowl with the rest of the ingredients. Adjust the seasonings. Ladle the soup into individual bowls, scatter some avocado over the top and add a dollop of yogurt. Garnish with chopped chives or a sprig of watercress. Serve with the remaining avocado and yogurt in separate bowls on the side. Serving the soup with the topping is only an option – it's great just on its own as well.

Chicken Soup with Meat Blintzes

Meat Blintzes

2–3 tablespoons chicken fat or cooking oil

1 onion, chopped

2 cups ground beef

salt and pepper

2–3 tablespoons chopped fresh parsley

Crêpes (recipe page 8)

extra oil or chicken fat for frying

This soup brings instant solace. I learned this version of chicken stock when I was in India, from a chef who ran a wonderful Chinese restaurant there. He used chicken carcasses to make the stock, which is superb.

Chicken Stock

4.4lb/2 kg chicken carcasses

2 bunches of celery

3 carrots

3 bay leaves

10–12 cups water

Place all the ingredients in a large pot and simmer for about 1½ to 2 hours. Strain the soup, allow to cool and gently spoon off any fat that has risen to the top. Another method is to place paper towels over the soup and allow them to absorb the fat. Repeat the process until all the fat is removed from the soup. Place back on heat and season with salt, pepper and powdered chicken stock, if desired.

Heat chicken fat or oil in frying pan. Cook onion till glossy. Add meat, season and cook till done. Allow to cool. Place a Crêpe on a work surface. Place a tablespoon of meat filling in the center of the Crêpe. Fold over all sides so that they overlap in the middle. Turn Crêpe over so that the loose ends are on the bottom. Use up all the filling in this way. Heat chicken fat or oil in frying pan about ¼"/1cm deep. Cook blintzes until golden brown on each side. Drain on paper towels.

Ladle chicken soup into bowls, add a meat blintz and some chopped parsley to garnish.

Magical Matzo Balls for Chicken Soup

Chicken soup with matzo balls really does have magical qualities. It's reputed to cure all illnesses and realign the brainwaves. My grandmother would never give anyone this recipe, with one exception, my aunt's cook Joseph. He then taught it to us. This is the inheritance my grandmother unwittingly left us, so treasure it. I do.

Neshoma Filling for Matzo Balls (Kneidlach)

2 tablespoons chicken fat or cooking oil

1 onion, chopped

4 tablespoons matzo meal

4 tablespoons sugar

1 egg, beaten

1 tablespoon cinnamon

salt to taste

Melt chicken fat/cooking oil in a frying pan. Cook onion till glossy. Add 2 tablespoons of the matzo meal and 2 tablespoons of sugar. Toss. Add the beaten egg, cinnamon and salt, adding equal amounts of matzo meal & sugar until the mixture becomes crumbly. Allow to cool. This freezes well.

Matzo Balls (Kneidlach)

The consistency of the matzo meal seems to change each year and can affect the amount you need to use and the time it takes to cook. When I first started to make Kneidlach, they would take 30 minutes and would be soft and perfect. These days, it can take up to an hour. Remember, the cardinal rule when making Kneidlach is: Do not open the lid for the first 40 minutes! This recipe is foolproof and in all the years I have been making them, I have never made a hard one.

3 tablespoons chicken fat or cooking oil

3 eggs

matzo meal

salt and pepper to taste

Heat a large pot of water with a little salt and bring to a boil. Place chicken fat or cooking oil and eggs in a mixing bowl and whisk together until they are well blended. Add a little matzo meal at a time, until the mixture starts to hold together. It must not be too stiff; allow it to be more on the moist side. Dampen your hands with water so that the mixture does not stick, and form into balls just larger than a golf ball. Bend your index finger and make an indent with the knuckle. Fill with about a teaspoon of the Neshoma Filling, and close the mixture around it, making sure there are no cracks.

When they are all done, place them immediately into the rapidly boiling water. Close the lid tightly. After 40 minutes, remove the lid and check the Kneidlach by lifting one out with a large spoon and gently pricking it with a fork. If the center is still firm, place the lid back on and allow to boil for a further 20 to 30 minutes, or until they are soft. Add more boiling water if some has evaporated. They can be reheated in the soup.

I'm in the Mood for

When I was first living in Los Angeles, mussel chowder appeared on many of the menus. I wanted to create my own recipe that would seduce the taste buds and take the words "mouth-watering" to another dimension. This was one of the first dishes I taught in my cooking school and it is as sensational now as it was then. I also make this soup as a peace offering when I know I have behaved particularly badly. No man can resist forgiving me!

2–3 tablespoons oil

2 onions, chopped

minced garlic to taste

3 potatoes, peeled and cubed

2 x 16oz/450g cans tomatoes, chopped

10 cups water + 2–3 tablespoons
  powdered chicken stock,
  or 10 cups homemade chicken stock

2 teaspoons oregano

2 teaspoons thyme

2 teaspoons rosemary

¼ teaspoon black pepper

½ teaspoon cayenne pepper

2 teaspoons salt

2–3 tablespoons brown sugar

1 cup canned clams

4 cups cooked mussels on the half shell

3 tablespoons freshly chopped parsley

Heat oil in a large saucepan. Cook onions with garlic till onions are glossy. Add potatoes, tomatoes, water and powdered stock (or homemade stock), and seasonings. Simmer for 1 hour. Add the clams with the juice. Rinse the mussels well and add with the parsley. Simmer for a further 30 minutes. Adjust seasonings and serve.

Mussel and Clam Chowder

Fooling Around
with Two-Tone

Soup

I was taken to Sunday lunch by my soon-to-be ex-husband and tasted the most delicious soup I had eaten for a very long time. The restaurant owner insisted that I try some and it was sensational. I went home with the flavor still lingering in my mouth and made a pot for myself. My son Mathew, who never eats soup and is one of my harshest cooking critics, loved it, and I have been making pots of it ever since.

This recipe looks fantastic and is seriously impressive. Use any combination of Curried Roasted Sweet Potato and Mango Soup, Red Pepper Soup and Creamed Watercress and Spinach Soup. Choose two and when they are ready follow the instructions on how to serve.

To Serve

Pour each of the soups into a jug with a spout. Holding a jug in each hand, gently pour the soups into a soup bowl so that they meet in the middle. Garnish with watercress, croutons, parsley or chives. Serve cream on the side.

Curried Roasted Sweet Potato & Mango Soup

4 sweet potatoes

3–4 tablespoons oil

3 leeks, white part only, or 3 onions, chopped

2 large mangoes or
　　1 x 16oz/450g can mangoes with the juice

8–10 cups water

1 tablespoon curry powder, or to taste

cayenne pepper to taste

salt to taste

1 cup milk (or cream)

Preheat oven to 350F/180C. Peel sweet potatoes and cut into wedges. Place on baking sheet and drizzle with oil. Roast in oven for about 30–40 minutes, turning them over as they cook so that they brown evenly.

Heat oil in large soup pot. Wash and chop leeks and cook till glossy. Peel and slice mangoes. Toss with leeks. Add roasted sweet potatoes and water. Simmer for 45 minutes. Strain the soup, retaining liquid, place vegetables in food processor and process until smooth. Add a little of the soup stock to make it easier to purée. Return to pot with the liquid and heat along with spices and milk (or cream). Simmer for 20 minutes, adjust seasonings and serve with heavy cream on the side (optional).

Red Pepper Soup

3 tablespoons butter plus 3 tablespoons oil

2 onions, chopped

4–6 red peppers, seeded and chopped

2 potatoes, peeled and cubed

2 cups sieved canned tomatoes

8–10 cups vegetable or chicken stock

salt, black pepper and brown sugar to taste

cream or buttermilk (optional)

Heat butter and oil in a large soup pot. If butter is omitted use 4–5 tablespoons oil. Cook onions till glossy. Add peppers and cook till slightly softened. Add potatoes, toss, add sieved tomatoes and stock and simmer for one hour. Strain and purée the vegetables, retaining the liquid. Return vegetables and liquid to pot, season and simmer for 20 minutes. Add cream or buttermilk to taste, or serve on the side.

Creamed Watercress & Spinach Soup

3 tablespoons butter plus 3 tablespoons oil

2 onions, chopped

2 bunches spinach

2 bunches watercress

2 potatoes, peeled and cubed

8–10 cups chicken or vegetable stock

salt and pepper to taste

cream or buttermilk to taste

Heat oil and butter or 4–5 tablespoons of oil if butter is omitted. Cook onions till glossy. Add spinach, watercress and potatoes. Add stock and allow soup to simmer for 1 hour. Strain, retaining liquid, and purée vegetables in food processor. Return vegetables and liquid to stove, season & simmer for 20 minutes. Add cream or buttermilk to taste, or serve on the side.

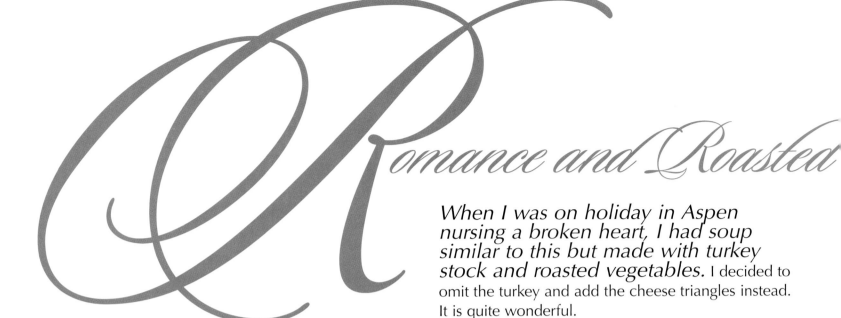

Romance and Roasted

When I was on holiday in Aspen nursing a broken heart, I had soup similar to this but made with turkey stock and roasted vegetables. I decided to omit the turkey and add the cheese triangles instead. It is quite wonderful.

4 tablespoons oil

3 onions, chopped

2 potatoes, peeled and cubed

6 zucchini, sliced lengthwise

2 medium eggplants, sliced, salted & allowed to stand for 30 minutes, then rinsed well

1 cup cauliflower, broken into flowerets

1 cup broccoli, broken into flowerets

8 summer squash/pattypans, quartered

4 leeks, white part only, sliced into rings

4 large carrots, sliced in half and quartered

10 cups water

1 tablespoon powdered chicken stock

4 cups sieved or chopped canned tomatoes

minced garlic to taste

salt, black pepper, cayenne pepper and brown sugar to taste

Preheat oven to 350F/180C degrees. Heat 4 tablespoons oil in a large soup pot. Cook onions till glossy. Add potatoes and toss for a few minutes. Place the rest of the vegetables on a baking sheet. Drizzle with oil and sprinkle with salt and pepper. Roast vegetables for about an hour or until they start to brown slightly. Add them to the pot with onions and potatoes. Add water, powdered chicken stock, tomatoes, & seasonings. Allow to simmer for 40 minutes. Adjust seasonings. Ladle into soup bowls, place a Phyllo Cheese Triangle on top of the soup and a sprig of watercress. Serve.

Vegetable Soup with Phyllo Cheese Triangles

Phyllo Cheese Triangles

1 cup grated mozzarella cheese

½ cup feta cheese, crumbled

¼ cup Parmesan cheese

2 teaspoons Italian dressing

salt and pepper to taste

1 package phyllo pastry

¼ cup butter, melted

sesame seeds for sprinkling

Preheat oven to 350F/180C. Place all the cheese and seasonings in a bowl and combine well. Using one sheet of phyllo pastry at a time, brush with melted butter and cut into 4 equal rectangles. Place about 2 teaspoons of cheese mixture at the top end of each rectangular strip of pastry and fold the same way you would fold a flag to form a triangular shape. Place on a greased baking sheet, brush with more melted butter and sprinkle with sesame seeds. Bake for about 20 minutes or until golden brown. These are delicious served with drinks as well.

Steamy Minestrone Soup with Pesto

My mother and I once spent three weeks in Nice where we ate vegetable soup with a dollop of pistou. It was so good we ate it nearly every night. It inspired me to make this Minestrone Soup with Pesto, which is a killer combination and a wonderful way to begin the journey into his heart.

4 tablespoons oil

1 cup onions, chopped

minced garlic to taste

4 potatoes, peeled and cubed

4 cups Italian tomatoes, sieved or chopped

6–8 cups chicken stock

salt, black pepper, cayenne pepper,
   brown sugar to taste

2 teaspoons oregano

2 teaspoons thyme

1 cup frozen corn

1 cup fresh broccoli

1 cup fresh cauliflower

1 can beans of your choice

1 cup cooked small shell pasta
   (or any small pasta)

Put oil into large soup pot and heat. Cook onions with garlic till onions are glossy. Add potatoes and toss. Cook for a few minutes. Add the tomatoes and chicken stock. Add seasonings. Allow to simmer for about 1 hour. Add corn, broccoli and cauliflower. Simmer for another half hour. Add beans and pasta. Heat through. Serve with a dollop of Pesto (recipe page 69).

Sensuous Discoveries

Salads & Vegetables

For me, Sundays in summer mean a table laden with wonderful, brightly coloured salads, and watching my muscled lover standing over the barbecue in the hot sun, imagining what I am going to do to him once the guests have left.

Say it with Salad Dressings

Choose any of the following salad dressings to serve with the salads, depending on your mood. You can also experiment using different exotic oils. If you like garlic, add either one crushed clove or ¼ teaspoon bottled minced garlic.

Honey Mustard Vinaigrette

1 cup oil

½ cup white or balsamic vinegar (the mustard seeds show up better using white vinegar)

2 teaspoons mustard powder

1 heaped tablespoon pommery or seeded mustard

1 tablespoon honey

1 tablespoon tangy mayonnaise

minced garlic to taste

1 teaspoon salt, sprinkling of black pepper

Whisk all ingredients together and adjust seasonings. Adding a tablespoon of Tahini Sauce (recipe page 143) to this is a great variation.

Paprika Honey Vinaigrette

1 cup oil

½ cup vinegar

1 heaped tablespoon pommery (seeded) mustard

2 teaspoons dry mustard (optional)

1 tablespoon honey

2 teaspoons paprika

minced garlic to taste

1 teaspoon salt

dash of black pepper

Place all the ingredients in a food processor and blend until smooth.

Hazelnut Vinaigrette

Use the above recipe and add 1 cup of hazelnuts. Place all the ingredients in a food processor and blend until smooth. Macadamia nuts are another great alternative.

Herbed Vinaigrette

1 cup oil

½ cup vinegar

1 tablespoon sugar

2 teaspoons mustard powder

few drops Tabasco sauce

2 teaspoons finely chopped scallions

2 teaspoons oregano

2 teaspoons thyme

minced garlic to taste

1 teaspoon salt

dash of black pepper

Place all the ingredients in a food processor and blend until smooth.

Homemade Mayonnaise

This is my mother's recipe and was the first thing I ever learned to make. I was 20 years old and on my honeymoon. It's not only the best mayonnaise I have ever eaten, but it outlived the marriage. IT still gets to sit at my table!

4 extra large eggs

4 teaspoons mustard powder

8 tablespoons white vinegar

1 tablespoon sugar

1 teaspoon salt

dash of pepper

4 cups oil

Place all ingredients except the oil in food processor. Measure oil into a beaker and very slowly pour down the funnel while the motor is running. Process until thickened. Check seasonings and store in fridge.

Roquefort Dressing

1 cup Roquefort cheese

1 cup Homemade Mayonnaise

2 tablespoons tangy mayonnaise

2 teaspoons anchovy paste

4 scallions

¼ cup vinegar

salt, black pepper and sugar to taste

Place all the ingredients in a food processor and mix well. Adjust seasonings. If too thick, add a little vinegar.

Balsamic Vinaigrette Dressing

1 cup oil

½ cup balsamic vinegar

2 teaspoons dry mustard powder

1 teaspoon sugar

minced garlic to taste

1 teaspoon minced ginger (optional)

1 teaspoon salt

½ teaspoon black pepper

Place all the ingredients in a food processor and blend until smooth.

Recklessly Wild Rice

This was a salad I dedicated to one of my men who loved rice and smoked chicken. Unlike the man, this recipe has never reached its expiry date.

Many of these salads may be served as a starter as well as an accompaniment to a main course. I either serve them on big platters or on individual plates, or in between courses when I need extra time to get the next dish prepared.

2 cups mushrooms, sliced
Salad Dressing of your choice (recipes page 40)
2 cups brown rice
1 cup wild rice
smoked chicken, skin and bones removed
4 stalks celery, chopped
4 scallions, chopped
1 cup walnuts, chopped and toasted
salt and pepper to taste
lettuce for garnishing

Place mushrooms in a bowl and marinate in Salad Dressing for 30 minutes. Cook each rice separately according to instructions on package – wild rice takes longer to cook. Rinse and cool. Mix mushrooms and rices together, season with salt, black pepper and more Salad Dressing. Pile in the center of a serving bowl. Cut chicken into strips or bite-size pieces and scatter over rice. Top with celery, scallions and walnuts. Break off pieces of lettuce and surround the edges of the rice mound. Serve.

and Chicken Salad

Bread Stick Salad Bliss with Caramelized Pears, Roquefort and Sugared Pine Nuts

1 tablespoon sugar

2 tablespoons butter

2 pears, sliced thinly

assortment of salad greens

1 cup cherry tomatoes

1 English cucumber, sliced

1 cup sugar snap or snow peas, blanched

1 cup baby corn, blanched

1 red and 1 yellow pepper, cut into julienne
strips

1 package baby carrots

½–1 cup Roquefort cheese, crumbled

1 cup pine nuts, toasted

2 tablespoons sugar

Heat sugar and butter together over high heat until it just begins to caramelize. Add the pears and toss till they soften and are well coated with the caramel. In another pan, heat the pine nuts and sugar over high heat. Gently stir until the sugar begins to melt and coat the nuts. Place on a baking sheet to cool. Break into pieces and set aside. (These freeze well).

Set out salad ingredients on a large platter or on individual salad plates. Lean Bread Sticks over the mound of salad so that they form a steeple around the platter. Drizzle Cranberry Dressing on top, add Roquefort cheese and scatter pine nuts. Serve.

My second husband, Icicle, once took me to New York for the Christmas holidays. We stayed with friends of his on a beautiful estate on Long Island. One Sunday, we lunched at a restaurant where I ate a salad that inspired this recipe.

Bread Sticks

1 package puff pastry

1 egg, beaten

1 cup cheddar cheese, grated

fresh Parmesan cheese

Preheat oven to 350F/180C. Roll out puff pastry and cut into ½"/1cm strips. Brush with egg and then sprinkle with cheeses. Twist two pastry strips together, pinching each end firmly together, and place on a greased baking sheet. Bake for about 20 minutes or until golden brown. Will keep in airtight container for a few days.

Cranberry Dressing

1 cup oil

½ cup balsamic vinegar

1 teaspoon sugar

2 teaspoons mustard powder

2 tablespoons cranberry jelly

1 teaspoon salt

minced garlic and black pepper to taste

Place ingredients in food processor and process until smooth. Add a little water to thin. Check seasonings and refrigerate.

Voluptuous Feta Salad

Amounts may vary, depending on the number of people at your table.

Use a combination of salad greens and a variety of vegetables, such as:

> tomatoes cut into quarters
>
> English cucumbers sliced into circles or half-moon shapes
>
> baby carrots
>
> chopped scallions
>
> red peppers
>
> steamed snow peas
>
> Kalamata olives
>
> Danish feta cheese is delicious but if unavailable, black peppered feta would be my second choice. Cut it into cubes and taste it for saltiness – rinse under cold water if it is too salty.

Deep fry the following vegetables in batches until crispy, drain on paper towels and set aside:

> 1 large sweet potato, peeled and julienned
>
> 2 carrots, peeled and julienned
>
> 3-4 leeks, white part only, sliced into matchstick pieces

Using a large platter, pile the salad greens down the center, making sure it's highest in the middle. Scatter the vegetables and feta cheese cubes around the edges of the greens. Gently place the deep-fried vegetables on top of the greens, drizzle with a Salad Dressing of your choice (recipes page 40) and serve.

This salad is a definite winner and has the ability to dazzle everyone. I was working in a sandwich shop in Beverly Hills when Elizabeth Taylor's head of security came in and ordered it. Less than an hour later I received a call from her assistant asking me to cater Ms. Taylor's Oscar® dinner. I had just landed my first client in Los Angeles!

Risqué Roasted Vegetable

This is one of my favorite salads. Roasted Vegetables have taken the world by storm. They are served everywhere, and with everything. Use your own selection of vegetables, but try using ones that are colorful. I generally use:

Roasted Vegetables

½ lb/250g string beans
½ lb/250g zucchini
½ lb/250g yellow summer squash/pattypans
2 medium eggplants

Slice the zucchini lengthways into four and cut the squash in quarters. Slice the eggplants into thin slices and sprinkle with salt to bleed for ½ hour. Then rinse well. Preheat the oven to 350F/180C. Place all the vegetables on a baking sheet, drizzle with cooking or olive oil and sprinkle with salt and pepper. Roast for about 45 minutes or until they are slightly tender and spotted with brown marks. You may want to splash balsamic vinegar over them while they are still hot, or mix some with the oil before roasting. Drizzling Tabasco sauce over them gives a terrific kick.

Salad

assortment of salad greens, including arugula
several fresh basil leaves
1 English cucumber, sliced
½ lb/250g cherry tomatoes,
   or 4 tomatoes, sliced
2 red peppers, seeded and julienned
4 carrots, julienned
1 cup sun-dried tomatoes, sliced
Parmesan cheese
Salad Dressing of your choice (recipes page 40)
fresh basil to garnish

Make a thin omelette using 2 eggs beaten with a little milk. Allow to cool. Roll up and slice into ½"/1cm strips. Set aside.

Arrange salad greens on a platter. Scatter the roasted vegetables and the sun-dried tomatoes on top and then place the omelette strips in a lattice pattern around the borders of the salad. Using a vegetable peeler, make Parmesan shavings and place all over the salad. Drizzle with Salad Dressing, garnish with a sprig of basil & serve.

Salad with Parmesan Shavings

Caramelized Butternut Squash

2–3 cups diced butternut squash

2–3 tablespoons oil or butter
   or a combination of both

salt and brown sugar for sprinkling

Heat oven to 350F/180C. Place butternut in an ovenproof dish and drizzle with oil or top with knobs of butter. Sprinkle with salt and brown sugar. Bake for about 45 minutes or until the brown sugar caramelizes slightly.

I made up a version of this popular salad, that I first tasted in California, and taught it in my cooking school in South Africa. It became a huge hit. I often make this salad without the chicken, adding julienne strips of carrots, steamed baby corn and snow peas. I have also made it by substituting smoked trout and smoked salmon for the chicken. It's always sensational.

1 package cellophane noodles, also known as rice noodles

oil for deep frying

roast chicken, de-boned and flaked

1 bunch scallions, chopped

sesame seeds, toasted

1 cup flaked almonds, toasted

lettuce

Heat oil in a large frying pan suitable for deep-frying. Break the cellophane noodles into manageable pieces. Test the temperature of the oil by dropping one rice noodle in. The oil is hot enough when the noodle bounces to the top and puffs up. If it sinks, the oil is not hot enough. Deep-fry the noodles quickly, turning them over as soon as the first side is done. Drain on paper towels.

Place noodles on a large platter, and arrange the lettuce to frame the noodles. Scatter the chicken, scallions, sesame seeds and flaked almonds over the noodles. Pour Sweet and Sour Dressing over salad and serve immediately.

Variation

I made a variation of this salad for Caviar the day he took me on a picnic to Zuma Beach in Malibu. I was in need of his hugs so he flew in for the day, rented a convertible and took me to the beach, where he showered me with hugs and kisses and I showered him with food. Since he loved it so much I can't resist sharing it.

shredded lettuce

5½ oz broken angel hair pasta

2 cups bean sprouts

2 cups roast chicken, sliced into strips

1 English cucumber, chopped

6 scallions, chopped

3 tablespoons sesame seeds

1 cup flaked almonds, toasted

cellophane noodles, deep fried

cilantro or parsley, chopped (optional)

Toss ingredients together, piling the cellophane noodles into a tower on top of the salad. Drizzle with Sweet and Sour Dressing and garnish with cilantro or parsley.

Shangri-La

Sweet & Sour Dressing

1 cup sunflower oil

½ cup vinegar or rice vinegar

½ cup sugar

1 teaspoon minced ginger (optional)

¼ cup soy sauce

2 teaspoons mustard powder,
   or 1 teaspoon Chinese mustard

1 tablespoon peanut butter

dash of salt and black pepper

Whisk ingredients together and pour over salad.

Titillating Tuna Steak

When I was divorcing my second husband, Icicle, I went off to Los Angeles to escape. I called my American Adonis, Caviar, and asked if he was free to meet me there. He was.

Caviar made all the arrangements, as usual. I collected the car he had booked for me and found my way to The Ritz Carlton where he had made a reservation. The hotel was fabulous. I jumped up and down on the bed, ran a bath and felt like I was breathing oxygen for the first time in months.

I picked up Caviar at the airport the following morning. He was as beautiful as ever and we fell into each other's arms. We went into Santa Monica and walked around, cuddling under an umbrella in the light drizzle. After a while we found a restaurant and I had a tuna steak salad that was absolutely delicious – and left me wanting more.

The memory of that lunch and the afternoon in bed was so glorious that I had to create a recipe to mark the day.

I've added Thai Vegetables to give it an extra zing. Any of my Vinaigrette Dressings will work well with this recipe.

> 1 tuna steak per person
> lemon juice and olive oil
>   and black pepper for marinade

Marinate tuna steaks for an hour in lemon juice, olive oil and black pepper.

Salad Ingredients

Use the following approximate quantities per plate:

> 6–8 cherry tomatoes
> 4–6 sun-dried tomatoes
> a few slices English cucumber
> 6–8 julienned slices red pepper
> 2 scallions, chopped
> 5 slivers avocado
> 2–3 boiled new potatoes, cut in half
> variety of salad greens

Arrange salad ingredients decoratively on individual plates, piling the greens in the middle. Heat a steak pan, season the tuna steaks with salt and sear them for a few minutes on each side. The tuna should be pink inside. Drizzle Vinaigrette Dressing (recipes page 40) over salad ingredients, place tuna steak on top of greens & then top with about two tablespoons of Thai Vegetables. Serve.

Thai Vegetables

1 cup finely shredded cabbage

1 cup each, carrots, red peppers, cucumbers, julienned

1 tablespoon chopped cilantro

2 teaspoons lemon grass, chopped (or bottled variety)

lemon juice, salt, pepper, crushed dried chili, sugar to taste

Combine all the vegetables together. Splash with lemon juice; season with salt, pepper, fresh or dried chilies or chili paste and sugar. Allow vegetables to marinate 15–30 minutes before serving.

Melting Mashed

The first time I traveled first class to Europe, the food they served on the plane was superb. I had something similar to this and it forever elevated mashed potatoes to a place deserving of respect. These not only look impressive, they are delicious.

> 2–3 tablespoons butter
> 4–6 potatoes, boiled
> milk, salt and pepper
> 1 package phyllo pastry
> ½ –1 cup butter, melted

Heat 2–3 tablespoons butter in a pot. Add potatoes, a little milk, salt and pepper. Reduce heat. Using potato masher, mash until smooth, adding more milk and butter to make a light fluffy consistency. Correct seasonings.

Brush one sheet of phyllo pastry with melted butter. Fold in half, brush with more melted butter and fold in half again to form a square. Brush with more melted butter. Spoon a tablespoon of mashed potatoes in the center of the pastry. Bring the sides of the pastry up to meet in the middle above the potato. Using melted butter, press the edges together to close the parcel. Brush with more melted butter. Bake in a preheated 350F/180C oven for 20 minutes or until golden brown. Adding 2 to 3 tablespoons of pesto, freshly grated nutmeg or chopped sun-dried tomatoes to the mashed potatoes is also delicious.

The most frequent requests from women who attend my cooking classes are for interesting & delicious vegetable dishes to impress their men. Of course I can oblige! A good vegetable accompaniment elevates a meal to another dimension.

Potatoes Hugged in Phyllo

Irresistible Indian Tortillas

oil for cooking and deep frying

1 onion, chopped

minced garlic to taste

2 potatoes, boiled and cubed

½ cup cooked lentils

1 cup string beans, steamed and cut in half

1 eggplant

1 cup summer squash/pattypan, quartered

3 zucchini, chopped

1 cup sieved tomatoes

2 tablespoons curry powder

1–2 tablespoons brown sugar

salt, pepper, cayenne pepper to taste

2 cups soy flour
    mixed to a paste with cold water

1 package pappadums

Yogurt Sauce

chutney

Heat 2 tablespoons oil and cook onion and garlic until onion is glossy. Slice and salt the eggplant and allow to bleed for half an hour. Rinse well. Add vegetables to the onions and cook for a few minutes. Add the sieved tomatoes and seasonings and allow to simmer for 30 minutes. Adjust seasonings.

Place soy paste in a metal colander over hot oil (about 2"/5cm deep) and push the paste through with the back of a spoon. Keep separating them as they cook so that they do not form into one mass. When the flakes of dough are golden brown, remove and drain on paper towels. If some pieces are too big, break them up after they have cooled.

Cook pappadums in 1"/3cm of oil, ensuring that they cook fairly flat (hold down with two spoons). Place a pappadum in the center of each plate. Heap the curried vegetables on top. Scatter the soy flakes generously over the vegetables and drizzle with Yogurt Sauce and chutney.

Yogurt Sauce

1 cup yogurt

2 tablespoons finely chopped mint

1 chili, chopped

salt to taste

Mix yogurt with mint, chili and salt to taste and set aside.

Whenever Caviar and I get together we go on eating orgies. One of the many things I love about him is the way he takes care of everything. I don't even have to look at the menu because he knows exactly what to order. We both love hot food so on this night in London he chose a beautiful Indian restaurant where I had the best Indian food I have ever eaten. We sat staring into each other's eyes, eating nearly everything on the menu and oohhing and aahhing our way through it. This is similar to one of the dishes we had that night.

Tickled & Pickled Peppers and Cucumbers

When I open my fridge and see these sitting there, I know my day will be just fine.

Pickled Cucumbers

- 3 English cucumbers
- 2½ cups water
- 2½ cups vinegar
- 1½ cups sugar
- 3 teaspoons mustard seeds
- 8 peppercorns
- 4 bay leaves

Cut cucumbers into ½″/2cm slices. Put rest of ingredients in a large pot & heat until sugar dissolves. Add cucumbers, cover and simmer for 10 minutes. Cool. Store in a tightly sealed container in the fridge for 2 days before serving.

Pickled Peppers

- 12 peppers (I prefer using only red and yellow)
- 5 cups water
- 1½ cups vinegar
- 1½ cups sugar
- 1–2 crushed dried chilies or chopped fresh chilies (optional)

Cut peppers into ½″/2cm strips. Put rest of ingredients in a large pot and heat until sugar dissolves. Add peppers, cover and simmer for about 10 minutes. Cool. Store in a tightly sealed container in the fridge for 2 days before serving.

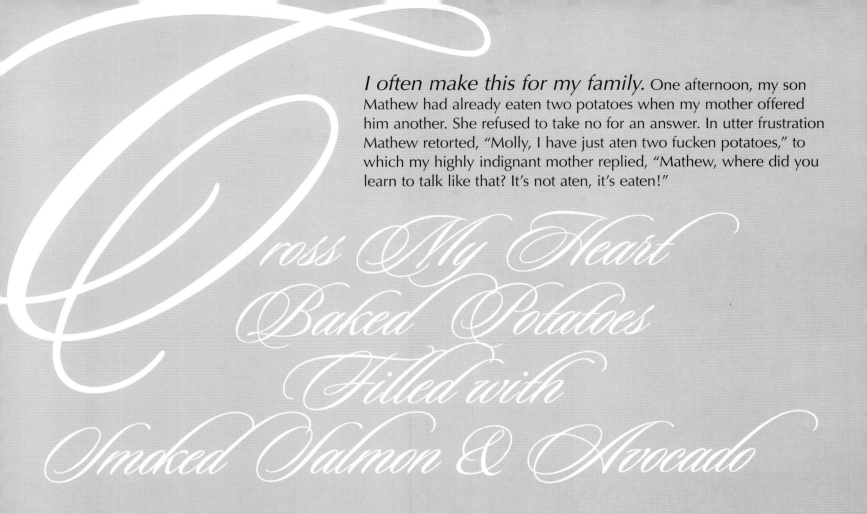

I often make this for my family. One afternoon, my son Mathew had already eaten two potatoes when my mother offered him another. She refused to take no for an answer. In utter frustration Mathew retorted, "Molly, I have just aten two fucken potatoes," to which my highly indignant mother replied, "Mathew, where did you learn to talk like that? It's not aten, it's eaten!"

Cross My Heart Baked Potatoes Filled with Smoked Salmon & Avocado

1 large potato per person

1 cup sour cream
   or Philadelphia cream cheese (optional)

smoked salmon

slices of avocado

Paprika Honey Vinaigrette

Preheat oven to 400F/200C. Wash potatoes well. Bake for about 1 hour or until skin is crispy. You may cook them in the microwave first to speed up the process and then crisp them in the oven. On the top of the potato cut two crossed lines on the diagonal, crossing in the middle (only cutting a third of the way down) and squeeze the sides gently so that some of the potato pushes out. Place a dollop of sour cream or cream cheese in the potato (if using) or just top with lashings of smoked salmon and thick slices of avocado. Serve Paprika Honey Vinaigrette (recipe page 40) on the side.

Filling

1 onion, chopped

3–4 tablespoons oil

2 cups spinach, chopped

1½ cups diced sweet potatoes

1½ cups diced butternut squash

salt and brown sugar to taste

1 cup buttermilk

2 eggs, beaten

1 cup Emmenthaler cheese, grated

salt and black pepper to taste

This creation, which is quite sensational, is for quiche lovers who would prefer something with no cream and far fewer eggs.

Pastry

1¾ cups flour

½ cup butter

1 egg yolk

juice of one lemon

enough cold water to form dough into a ball

Place all ingredients except water in a food processor. Mix until combined. Add the water while the motor is running, just until the dough forms into a ball.

Cook onion in oil until glossy. A combination of butter and oil may be used for a richer taste. Add spinach and toss till wilted. Place sweet potatoes and butternut squash on separate baking sheets, drizzle with oil. Season with salt and sprinkle brown sugar over the squash. Roast in a preheated 350F/180C oven until vegetables are tender.

Roll out dough and press into a 10"/26cm pie plate, and cover with wax paper. Bake (with paper) in a preheated 350F/180C oven for 10–15 minutes. Remove paper. Spread spinach over base. Combine buttermilk, beaten eggs, grated cheese & seasonings and pour over spinach. Spread squash and sweet potatoes on top. Bake for another 30 minutes or until set.

Sweet Potato & Butternut Flan

Woo Me with Wild Rice Stir Fry

1 cup brown or white rice

½ cup wild rice

oil for cooking

assortment of vegetables, using all
  or any of your choice of –

1 cup mushrooms

3 zucchini

1–2 red peppers

1 cup baby corn

1 cup sugar snap or snow peas

1 cup string beans

1 cup summer squash/pattypan

1 eggplant

salt and pepper to taste

3 tablespoons fresh chopped parsley

Cook each rice separately according to package instructions, remembering that wild rice takes longer to cook. Heat 3–4 tablespoons oil (may add a knob of butter) in a frying pan and cook vegetables. Steam hard vegetables like squash, zucchini, string beans first – but be careful not to overcook them. If using eggplants, they are much nicer if they are grilled first rather than steamed. They must first be salted and allowed to sit for 30 minutes to bleed. Rinse well. Add cooked rice, adding more oil if necessary, and season.

See Me, Feel Me, Touch Me, Tempt Me

What woman doesn't dream about sitting opposite a tall, dark & gorgeous man, with candlelight flickering, sipping wine and twirling pasta in a rich sauce into her mouth and being told by his eyes that she is more delectable than the food?

Passion-filled Panzerotti

This is erotica at its best – soft pillows packed with orgasmic power.

Pasta

Serves 6-8

> 1 cup flour
> 2 extra large eggs, beaten

Mix flour with beaten eggs. If you do not have a pasta machine, place on work surface and roll out very thinly. Use a glass to press out shapes. Roll each shape again as dough springs back when cut. The dough must be very thin. (You should almost be able to read a newspaper through it!)

Butternut Squash & Ricotta Filling

Whenever I have some of this mixture left over, I keep it to toss with penne or use it as a filling between sheets of lasagna pasta

> 2 cups diced butternut squash
> 1 cup ricotta cheese
> salt, black pepper, brown sugar
>   and nutmeg to taste

Steam squash. Drain. Purée along with ricotta cheese in a food processor. Season. There should be just a hint of nutmeg and the sugar gives it a lift.

Sugo Di Pomodoro

2 cups sieved Italian tomatoes
(process if using whole or chopped)

1 onion

salt, black pepper, touch of chili
or cayenne pepper & brown sugar to taste

cream

Place tomatoes, whole onion and seasonings in a saucepan and simmer for about 30 minutes. Adjust seasonings, remove onion and add a little cream to turn the sauce pink.

To Assemble

Brush the edges of dough with water. Place a teaspoon of the filling in the center of each circle of dough and fold over. Pinch the sides closed. They should be crescent-shaped. Repeat until all the filling and dough are used, about 15 panzerotti.

Boil a large pot of water with a little oil and cook until the panzerotti float to the top and are al dente. Drain well. Serve immediately while they are still puffy. Place 3-4 on each plate, spoon over some of the Sugo di Pomodoro, and scatter with freshly grated Parmesan cheese and black pepper. You are now ready to enter heaven.

Saucy Cheeses Over Roasted Vegetables

Serves 6-8

My Italian sister-in-law Toni made this pasta dish for her birthday & I could not stop eating it. Even thinking about it now makes my mouth water. The way she roasts vegetables makes this dish a gastronomical delight. I made it the very next day for my newest conquest and he, too, thought it quite out of this world.

assortment of vegetables, including –

1 eggplant

3–4 zucchini

4 celery stalks

1 cup string beans

1 cup summer squash/pattypan,
   cut into quarters

1 cup diced butternut squash

1 cup sliced mushrooms

2 leeks, sliced

red and yellow peppers cut into julienne strips

oil

balsamic vinegar

Tabasco sauce

salt and pepper

1lb/500g penne or other short pasta

4oz/100g Gorgonzola cheese

2 heaped tablespoons
   Philadelphia cream cheese

4–5 tablespoons Parmesan cheese

Preheat oven to 350F/180C. Slice the eggplants, salt them and allow to stand for half an hour. Rinse well and roughly chop. Dice all the other vegetables into thin slices or small chunks. Place on a baking sheet and drizzle with oil. Splash with balsamic vinegar and Tabasco sauce. Season with salt and pepper. Roast until speckled with brown spots.

Cook pasta according to instructions on package. Drain, reserving liquid, but do not rinse. While the pasta is still hot, fold in the Gorgonzola and cream cheese and add just enough liquid from the pasta so that the mixture is not stiff. Fold in the roasted vegetables. Season with salt and black pepper. Scatter with Parmesan and toss again. Serve, and feel your mouth smile and your breath escape in a sensuous sigh.

Love in The Shell With Mussels

I prepared this dish for Nelson Mandela when friends of mine invited him to dinner and they asked me to do the catering. I am a great fan of Mr. Mandela but unlike most of the world I have had the opportunity to cook for him, bake his welcome cake when he moved into his new home, and also to kiss him. He was being interviewed on a talk show and I was invited to sit in the audience. The talk show host asked me to come up on stage and give Mr. Mandela a kiss. Well, all I can say is, I was completely finished!

Serves 6–8
I often serve this as a main course in a paella pan using three different colored pastas. I arrange each color into an individual triangle to form 1/3 of a circle.

This is wonderful to serve with drinks as well. Place a bowl of the sauce in the center of a large platter surrounded with mussels on the half shell. Dip a mussel into the sauce and tilt it into his mouth. I guarantee you'll both spend the rest of the evening in heaven.

1lb/500g linguini
1lb/500g mussels, cooked on the half shell

Boil a pot of water. Add linguini and cook al dente. (Tossing pasta with two forks while it cooks improves the texture.) Rinse mussels well. If using uncooked mussels with both shells, clean well, steam them and discard the ones that do not open.

3 tablespoons butter
minced garlic to taste
¼ cup white wine
1 cup Neapolitane Sauce (recipe page 69)
1 cup mussel meat, cooked
3 tablespoons chopped parsley
salt and black pepper to taste

Melt butter in a saucepan and add garlic. Pour in the wine and sizzle for 1–2 minutes. Add Neapolitane Sauce. Heat and add mussels, parsley and seasonings. Toss with pasta.

Naughty But Oh So Nice Neapolitane Sauce

Serves 6–8

While women might think pasta equals romance, and men probably think pasta equals a satisfying meal, there's something about Italian food that compels both diners to head straight for the bedroom!

3–4 tablespoons oil

1 onion, grated

1 carrot, grated

½ red pepper, grated

2–3 bay leaves

4 cups sieved Italian tomatoes

salt, pepper, cayenne pepper
   and brown sugar to taste

fresh, dried or minced chili to taste

2 tablespoons Pesto

1 tablespoon butter (optional)

stock or water

Heat oil in a large saucepan. Cook onion, carrot, red pepper and bay leaves until glossy. Add tomatoes and spices and simmer for 30 minutes. Add Pesto, butter and a little stock or water if too thick. Add enough brown sugar to cut the acid in the tomatoes.

Pesto

1 cup fresh basil

1 cup cashew nuts
   (if using salted do not add extra salt)

¼ cup grated Parmesan cheese

minced garlic to taste

salt, black pepper to taste

oil

Put basil, nuts, cheese, garlic and seasonings in a food processor and process. While the motor is running add a little oil, just enough to bind the mixture. Adjust seasonings. Place in a covered container in the fridge or freezer.

Pasta al Forno con Amore

Serves 6–8

This is another sensational pasta dish. Add any vegetables of your choice – whatever you use will be delicious.

1lb/500g short pasta – penne, farfalle or fusilli – cooked al dente, drained but not rinsed

1½ cups Sugo di Pomodoro (recipe page 65)

Roasted Vegetables

Roasted Vegetables

Preheat oven to 350F/180C. Use any combination of your favorite vegetables, including 1 cup diced butternut squash, 2 red or yellow peppers and 1 cup carrots cut into julienne strips, 3–4 zucchini cut into quarters, 1 eggplant, sliced, salted and allowed to stand for 30 minutes and then rinsed and diced, 1 cup sliced mushrooms, 1 cup string beans and 3 celery sticks chopped. Drizzle with oil, season with salt and pepper and bake until speckled with brown spots.

White Sauce

3–4 tablespoons oil or butter, or combination of both

1 heaped tablespoon flour

½ cup milk

1 cup water

1 teaspoon powdered chicken stock (optional)

½ cup grated mozzarella cheese

½ cup grated Parmesan cheese

1–2 teaspoons powdered mustard

salt, black pepper

Heat oil. Sprinkle flour over top. Remove from heat and add milk, water and powdered stock (if using). Use a whisk and mix well. Place back on heat and, using the whisk, stir until smooth. Add cheese, mustard, salt and pepper. Add Sugo di Pomodoro. Adjust seasonings.

Preheat oven to 350F/180C. Place cooked pasta in an ovenproof dish along with the vegetables and the sauce. Mix well. Bake for about 20 minutes and serve.

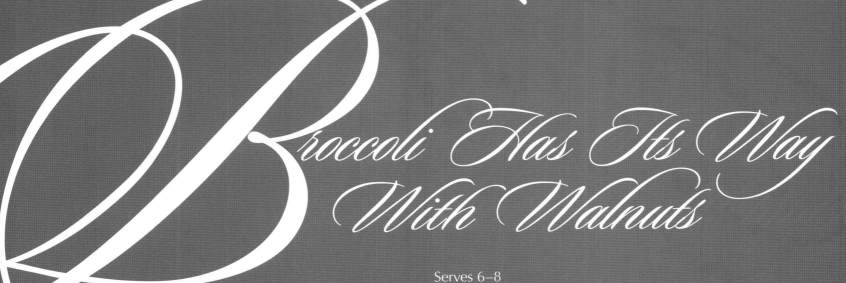

Broccoli Has Its Way With Walnuts

Serves 6–8

My younger son Jamie, who loves broccoli, was thrilled when I made this for him. My second husband, Icicle, who turned his nose up when he saw the ingredients, tried one helping and then asked for another!

2 tablespoons butter

½ cup low fat Philadelphia cream cheese

¼ cup grated Parmesan cheese

¼ cup milk or cream

1lb/500g good quality spaghetti, cooked al dente

2 cups broccoli flowerets, steamed

2 tablespoon Pesto (recipe page 69)

salt, black pepper and cayenne pepper to taste

1 cup coarsely chopped toasted walnuts

Heat the butter in a saucepan. Add the cream cheese, Parmesan and milk or cream. Stir to a smooth consistency, adding more milk or cream if necessary. Add the spaghetti and coat well. Add the broccoli, Pesto and seasonings and toss until well combined. Scatter the toasted walnuts over the pasta and serve with cracked black pepper and freshly grated Parmesan cheese.

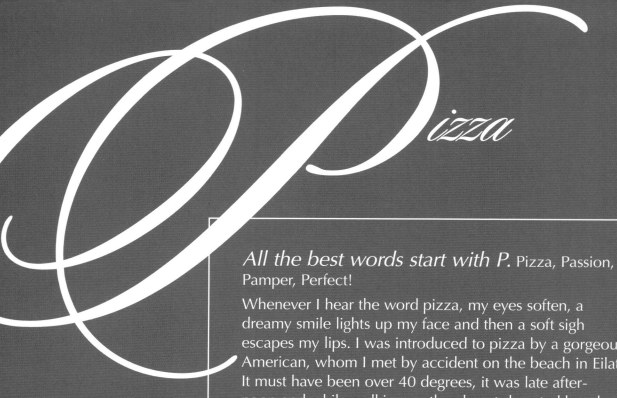

Pizza

All the best words start with P. Pizza, Passion, Pamper, Perfect!

Whenever I hear the word pizza, my eyes soften, a dreamy smile lights up my face and then a soft sigh escapes my lips. I was introduced to pizza by a gorgeous American, whom I met by accident on the beach in Eilat. It must have been over 40 degrees, it was late afternoon and while walking on the almost deserted beach, I noticed a tall, dark, beautiful man with a body like Michelangelo's David. My heart leaped, I felt the blood rush to my face and had difficulty breathing. This was Caviar, who would become my American Adonis.

I visited him in the United States a few months later and we spent much of our time eating our way along the West Coast. I fell in love with America, reveled in the food and of course completely fell for Caviar. Sixteen years later, he remains a very dear and loving friend who never fails to encourage me in pursuing my culinary interests.

Basic Perfection

Pizza Base

Baking the dough directly on a pizza stone gives it a wonderful crispy texture.

- 3 cups bread flour
  (cake flour may also be used)
- 1 package fast rising instant yeast
- 1½ teaspoons salt
- 2 tablespoons oil
- 1½ tablespoons honey
- 1 cup warm water

Preheat oven to 400F/200C. Mix dry ingredients. Add liquids and knead well. Cover with plastic wrap and a dish-towel and allow to rise until doubled in bulk. Punch down and roll out on a piece of lightly greased foil that can be put directly on the rack in the oven. Roll it out fairly thinly to form a circle, turning back the edges about ¼"/1cm to form a ridge. This makes one huge pizza. You can always divide the dough to make smaller ones. Bake for 10 minutes or till slightly golden brown. Remove from oven and loosen the base from the foil so that it will not stick later. Add toppings.

Spicy Tomato Pizza Sauce

This is a quick version. You can also use Neapolitane Sauce (recipe page 69)

- 3–4 tablespoons oil
- 1 onion, chopped
- minced garlic to taste
- 3 cups sieved or chopped tomatoes
- salt, black pepper, cayenne pepper, chili paste, brown sugar to taste

Heat oil in saucepan. Cook onion and garlic until onion is glossy. Add tomatoes and seasonings and simmer for 20 minutes.

Pizza With Pizazz

Pizza Base

Preheat oven to 400F/200C. Prepare Pizza Base dough (recipe page 73). Break off a piece of dough the size of a golf ball. Break it into two and roll it out to form a long sausage. Place the strips over the base to form a cross in the center that divides the base into four triangles. Press the edges of the strips to the turned-back edges of the base. Bake for 10–15 minutes until just starting to brown.

This pizza looks sensational. Use any of your favorite combinations of toppings, making sure the colors look good.

> steamed spinach and feta cheese
>
> fried onions and Kalamata olives
>
> anchovies
>
> grated cheddar cheese
>
> ricotta cheese
>
> mozzarella cheese
>
> julienne strips of red and yellow peppers
>
> salami or pepperoni
>
> roasted vegetables
>
> sun-dried tomatoes

To Prepare

Spread Spicy Tomato Pizza Sauce (recipe page 73) over the four sections of the base and fill each of the triangles with a different filling. Instead of using mozzarella cheese on all four triangles, you may want to use cheddar or ricotta to add color and variety. I often use spinach and feta, salami and olives, roasted vegetables and sun-dried tomatoes, fried onions and olives. On one of the triangles I may use cheddar with sliced tomatoes with sun-dried tomatoes scattered over. Season with black pepper and oregano. Bake for about 20–30 minutes or until base is crispy.

In 4 Combinations

Dreamy Pizza Niçoise

He'll be dreaming about being with you in the south of France after eating this. Sometimes dreams come true!

Pizza Base (recipe page 73)

Spicy Tomato Pizza Sauce (recipe page 73)

4 cups grated mozzarella cheese

2 red peppers, julienned

1 8oz/225g package mushrooms sliced
   – oyster mushroom are delicious

salt, pepper and thyme to taste

1 package spinach, chopped,
   steamed and dried well

3 tins tuna, drained and flaked

1 cup Kalamata olives, pitted

2 onions, sliced thinly and placed in boiling
   water for a few minutes, then drained

1 avocado, sliced

4 hard-boiled eggs, quartered

parsley for garnishing

Preheat the oven to 400F/200C. Spread Spicy Tomato Pizza Sauce and cheese on Pizza Base. Cook red peppers in a little oil until glossy. Remove. In the same oil, cook mushrooms with a little salt, pepper and thyme just until the liquid is expelled. Drain. Arrange spinach on top of cheese. Scatter tuna, mushrooms, red peppers, olives and onions on top. Bake until the cheese is bubbling & the crust is crisp (about 10 minutes). Remove from oven and top with avocado, hard-boiled eggs and parsley. Serve. Each topping may also be placed in a circle around the pizza base, starting from the outer edge and moving inwards.

Pizza el Greco with Lamb, Feta & Mint

This pizza puts you in the mood for making love on a Greek island

Pizza Base (recipe page 73)

Spicy Tomato Pizza Sauce (recipe page 73)

4 cups grated mozzarella cheese

1½ cups feta cheese, crumbled

3 cups diced cooked lamb

1 cup pitted black olives

4 tablespoons fresh mint leaves, chopped, with extra leaves for garnishing

Preheat oven to 400F/200C. Spread Spicy Tomato Pizza Sauce over the base, sprinkle with cheese and bake till crispy (about 20 minutes). Add the meat and the olives and bake another 10 minutes. Sprinkle with fresh mint, garnish with whole mint leaves and serve.

If ever you need an unfair advantage to seal a romance, serve this pizza!

Pizza Base (recipe page 73)

Spicy Tomato Pizza Sauce (recipe page 73)

4 cups grated mozzarella cheese

black pepper, Italian herbs
   or oregano to taste

arugula leaves

2 cups smoked salmon

¾ cup pine nuts, toasted

shavings of Parmesan cheese

1 cup sun-dried tomatoes

Preheat oven to 400F/200C. Spread Spicy Tomato Pizza Sauce over Pizza Base. Scatter cheese on top of sauce. Sprinkle with black pepper and Italian herbs or oregano. Bake until bubbling and base is crisp (about 20 minutes). Remove from oven. Scatter arugula and thinly sliced smoked salmon on top, then toasted pine nuts and sun-dried tomatoes. Serve. Chopped avocado is also wonderful with this.

Pizza Indulgence with Smoked Salmon, Arugula & Pine Nuts

Cobb Salad

Use any 5 or more of the following of ingredients:

Pizza Base (recipe page 73)
Spicy Tomato Pizza Sauce (recipe page 73)
4 cups grated mozzarella cheese

Preheat oven to 400F/200C. Cover pizza base with Spicy Tomato Pizza Sauce & grated mozzarella cheese. Bake until cheese is bubbling and dough is cooked through (about 20 minutes). Top with Cobb Salad and serve immediately.

sun-dried tomatoes
avocado
smoked chicken, tuna or any meat
4 hard-boiled eggs, chopped
ricotta cheese
Kalamata olives, pitted
steamed spinach, squeezed of any liquid
feta cheese
black pepper and Italian herbs or oregano

Choose any five or more of the above and place each one in a circular pattern on the baked Pizza Base, starting from the outer edge and working towards the center. Season with salt, black pepper and herbs. Serve.

a Turn On Top

Pizza Perfecto with Roasted Vegetables

I once asked a boyfriend of mine what he considered the three sexiest foods. Without hesitating, he replied, "Pizza, ice cream and you." That was when I realized what a powerful aphrodisiac cooking could be.

Pizza Base (recipe page 73)

2 eggplants

6 zucchini, sliced lengthwise into four

6–8 yellow and green summer squash/ pattypans, cut into quarters

1 cup string beans

1 cup baby corn

1 cup sun-dried tomatoes

1–2 cups mushrooms, sliced

Spicy Tomato Pizza Sauce (recipe page 73)

4 cups grated mozzarella cheese

oregano and black pepper

Preheat oven to 350F/180C. Place all the vegetables except the eggplant on a baking sheet. Drizzle with oil and season with salt and pepper. Roast for 45 minutes or until speckled with brown spots. Slice the eggplant into rings. Sprinkle with salt and allow to stand for 30 minutes. Drain well. Place on a baking sheet, drizzle with oil and season with salt and pepper. Place under the broiler and watch carefully as they cook quickly and must be turned over when the first side is done.

Preheat the oven to 400F/200C. Spread Spicy Tomato Pizza Sauce over the base, sprinkle with cheese and bake until base is crispy (about 20 minutes). Add the vegetables and bake for another 10 minutes. Season with black pepper and oregano and serve.

Chapter Five

Reeling Them In

Seafood

**If you want a man to fall for you – hook, line and sinker –
nothing will impress him more than a sensational fish dish.**

South African fish are among the best in the world – Kingklip, Steenbras, Cape Salmon, Yellowtail or Sole. However, any firm whitefish, such as Halibut, Striped Sea Bass or Orange Roughy, are excellent substitutes.

Lure Him with Grilled Fish

I have yet to taste a better way to cook fish than this!

When grilling a whole fish, for best results make sure that it does not weigh more than 6.6 lbs/3kg. I prefer having the head and tail removed and the fish butterflied. Rinse and pat dry. Place on a greased baking sheet, skin side up. This also works just as well for fillets.

1 lemon

salt, black pepper

cajun spice (optional)

paprika

seafood seasoning or Accent

unseasoned breadcrumbs

butter or olive/vegetable oil

Splash lemon juice on the skin side of the fish. Season, sprinkle with breadcrumbs and dot generously with butter or drizzle with oil. Heat the broiler and place the fish on the highest rack next to the grill. Once the breadcrumbs have turned golden brown, turn the fish over, repeat seasoning procedure and grill again. Baste with pan juices while it's grilling and once again just before serving. Garnish with wedges or twists of lemon, sprinkle with parsley and serve immediately.

I often serve this on a platter surrounded with Woo Me With Wild Rice Stir Fry (recipe page 62). For dinner parties, grill one side earlier, turn the fish over & season. Then grill the other side just before you're ready to serve it.

Lover's Web of Spaghetti

Serves 6

4 pieces striped sea bass or any firm whitefish
juice of one lemon
salt, black pepper, paprika
seafood seasoning or Accent
unseasoned breadcrumbs
butter or olive oil for grilling

Heat broiler. Place fish on baking sheet. Squeeze a little lemon juice over fish and season. Sprinkle with breadcrumbs. Dot with knobs of butter or drizzle with oil. Place in oven right under grill. When breadcrumbs have turned golden brown, turn fish over and repeat seasoning procedure and grill. Slice into strips and set aside.

Spicy Neapolitane Sauce

½ lb spaghetti
3 tablespoons oil
1–2 chopped anchovies
½ cup pitted and chopped black olives
Neapolitane Sauce (recipe page 69)
cilantro or parsley to garnish
pine nuts to garnish

Cook spaghetti until al dente. Heat the oil in a saucepan and cook the anchovies with the olives for a few minutes. Add 2–3 cups of the Neapolitane Sauce. Add the cooked pasta (unrinsed) and toss. Add the fish to heat through. Using a barbecue fork, twirl the spaghetti around the fork and gently place in the center of each plate, piling it as high as it will stand. Sprinkle with cilantro or parsley and toasted pine nuts. Serve.

Striped Sea Bass
with Neapolitane Sauce
& Toasted Pine Nuts

Impulsive Prawns

Piri-piri is a term used in Portuguese cooking to describe something particularly hot and spicy. Exactly what will happen to your love life after taking a bite!

3 tablespoons butter

2 tablespoons oil

monosodium glutamate (MSG) or coarse salt

8–12 large prawns or tiger shrimp

juice of 1 lemon

salt, cayenne pepper, black pepper to taste

Heat butter and oil in a large frying pan. Sprinkle MSG or coarse salt lightly to cover bottom of pan. Add prawns and cook quickly, turning them over as they turn pink. Splash lemon juice over them and sprinkle with salt and cayenne and black pepper. Cook until second side is pink. Serve with Piri-Piri Sauce and rice stir-fried with chopped onions and red peppers.

Piri-Piri Sauce

3 tablespoons butter

2 tablespoons piri-piri oil

minced garlic to taste

juice of 1–2 lemons

salt, black pepper to taste

chili paste or minced chilies,
    cayenne pepper to taste

Put all ingredients in a saucepan. Heat through and adjust seasonings.

To Serve

Place rice in ramekin dish and unmold onto individual plates. Place the prawns decoratively around this, tail side up. Garnish with lemon baskets – cut 2 sections out of the top half of a lemon, leaving a strip intact as the "handle"; trim away the lemon and pith under the handle (as seen in picture on page 89).

Piri-Piri

*I had been living in Los Angeles
for six months, adamant that
I was finished with men.* And then
I met Better Than Chocolate and thought,
"Hmm, he looks nice." I agreed to go out
with him only because I had heard that he
loved to cook, which instantly elevated him
in my eyes.

He arrived at my apartment later that week to
cook dinner for me. He brought a cooler filled
with the most exotic ingredients, including a
fifty-year-old bottle of balsamic vinegar.
That did it! I was hooked. Here is the meal he
created for me. I hope it touches your taste
buds the same way he has touched my heart.

Fabulous Fish Barbecue

salmon fillet, one per person

maple syrup

salt and black pepper

cedar wood plank, one per person
 – bought in specialty food stores or from a
   lumber yard & cut into six ¼″ thick pieces

Soak the cedar wood in water for at least a half hour before using. Rub the salmon with a generous amount of maple syrup and season with salt and pepper. Place the salmon fillet on the cedar plank. Place on a hot barbecue, close the lid and allow to cook for about 15–20 minutes.

Cilantro Sauce

1 tablespoon oil

1 shallot

1 cup fresh cilantro

juice of 1 lemon

1 tablespoon honey

salt and black pepper

¼ cup rice vinegar

½ cup oil

Heat the tablespoon of oil in a saucepan. Brown shallot and then place in a preheated 400F/200C oven until soft. Place the shallot in a food processor along with the rest of the ingredients, except the oil, and blend well. While the motor is running, pour the oil slowly into the bowl until the mixture emulsifies. Adjust seasonings. Pour into a squeeze bottle and set aside.

Salad Dressing

½ cup olive oil

¼ cup lemon juice

¼ teaspoon minced garlic

½ teaspoon salt, dash of black pepper

1 teaspoon mustard powder

1 tablespoon honey

Whisk all ingredients together and set aside.

To Serve

1 cup pine nuts

2 tablespoons sugar

2 leeks, white part only

3 tablespoons oil

butter

assorted salad greens

Roquefort cheese

Toast the pine nuts in a saucepan with the 2 tablespoons of sugar, stirring until the sugar starts to stick to the nuts. Place toasted pine nuts on a baking sheet and when cooled, separate the nuts that have stuck together.

Slice the leeks into ½″ strips and sauté in 3 tablespoons oil and a nob of butter until soft.

Squeeze the cilantro sauce in a zigzag design across individual plates. Place a pile of leeks in the center of each plate, topped with a piece of salmon. Toss the salad greens well with the Salad Dressing and place a handful on top of the salmon. Crumble some Roquefort cheese over the salad and scatter with the sugared pine nuts. Serve.

Divine Grilled

This dish is a heavenly experience when shared with lovers and friends.

4 pieces any firm whitefish

juice of one lemon

salt, black pepper, paprika

seafood seasoning or Accent

unseasoned breadcrumbs

butter or olive oil for grilling

Heat broiler. Place fish on baking sheet. Squeeze a little lemon juice over fish and season. Sprinkle with breadcrumbs. Dot with knobs of butter or drizzle with oil. Place in oven right under grill. When breadcrumbs have turned golden brown, turn fish over and repeat seasoning procedure and grill.

Teriyaki Sauce

4 tablespoons soy sauce

4 tablespoons vinegar

½ cup water

just under ½ cup sugar

minced garlic to taste

1 tablespoon minced ginger

1–2 teaspoons potato flour or cornstarch mixed to a paste with a little water

2 tablespoons chopped cilantro

Place all the ingredients except the cilantro in a saucepan and simmer until it thickens slightly. Add cilantro.

To Serve

The way I often serve this is by placing a heap of sautéed spinach on the center of each plate, topped with mashed potatoes and then a piece of the grilled fish. Drizzle a little Teriyaki Sauce over the fish and then pile some cellophane noodles on top. Drizzle a little extra Teriyaki Sauce over the noodles and scatter with chopped cilantro.

Fish Teriyaki

Chapter Six

Birds of a Feather Sleep Together

I see the main course as "The Relationship." The neurotic part is over,
no more obsessing over a ringing telephone, and I can catch my breath after the chase.
What can compare to the luxurious feeling of having a pair of
gorgeous arms to sink into at the end of each day?

Chicken Teriyaki Kebabs Tucked into Pita with Tzatziki

This is one of my favorite sauces. I put it on everything from chicken to fish to stir-fries.

4 boneless chicken breasts
salt and pepper to taste
Teriyaki Sauce (recipe page 94)

Season chicken with salt and pepper. Soak kebab sticks in water for 30 minutes. Thread chicken onto the sticks. Pour Teriyaki Sauce over kebabs and marinate for a few hours or overnight.

Place kebabs on a baking sheet and drizzle with a little oil. Broil directly under the grill and baste while they are cooking. Turn them over when one side is cooked through. This is delicious served with heated pita bread and tzatziki. Prawns or tiger shrimp may be substituted for the chicken.

Stirring Chicken Stir Fry

in Phyllo
with Cilantro Sauce

Serves 6–8

When I cater for businessmen, I am repeatedly asked to prepare this dish. It can also be served as a starter – just make the phyllo rolls smaller. It's great with Teriyaki Sauce (recipe page 94) as well.

6 boneless chicken breasts, or 10 de-boned
    chicken thighs

Marinade

1 tablespoon soy sauce

1 tablespoon sherry

2 teaspoons cornstarch

1 egg white, lightly beaten

1 tablespoon ginger

½ teaspoon salt

Mix all Marinade ingredients together and allow chicken to marinate for at least 30 minutes.

3–4 tablespoons oil

minced garlic to taste

1–2 tablespoons fresh minced ginger

4 scallions, chopped

1–2 fresh or dried chilies (optional)

1 tablespoon sherry

1 cup each bok choy & Chinese cabbage

1 cup bean sprouts

1 cup string beans, chopped & lightly steamed

1 cup corn, fresh or frozen

1 cup canned water chestnuts, sliced

1 cup Chinese egg noodles
    broken into bite-size bits and cooked

3–4 tablespoons soy sauce

2 teaspoons sugar or honey

salt, black pepper to taste

dash of cayenne pepper

Heat oil in wok. Add garlic, ginger, scallions, chilies (if using) and chicken. Toss until chicken is cooked. Splash sherry over chicken, and cook for a further minute or two. Add the vegetables, egg noodles, soy sauce, honey and seasonings. Allow to cool completely before assembling. This dish may be served as it is without the phyllo pastry.

To Assemble

½ cup butter

1 package phyllo pastry

unseasoned breadcrumbs

sesame seeds

fresh cilantro

Melt the butter and brush one sheet of phyllo pastry. Place another sheet on top and brush with some more butter. Sprinkle some of the breadcrumbs over the sheets, fold in half, brush with more butter and sprinkle again with breadcrumbs. Place some of the cooled chicken mixture at the top of the rectangle – the short end (to form a thick sausage) – fold the sides of the pastry on either side going down the length, and then roll the pastry to form a parcel, keeping the sides tucked in. Brush the top with more melted butter and sprinkle with sesame seeds. Continue with the rest of the pastry in this way until all the chicken mixture has been used. Bake in a preheated 350F/180C oven for about 35–40 minutes or until golden brown.

Sauce

2 tablespoons soy sauce

1–2 teaspoons chili paste

1 tablespoon rice vinegar

1 cup chicken stock

1 tablespoon sherry

3 teaspoons sugar

2 teaspoons potato flour

1 tablespoon ground coriander

1 teaspoon honey

Combine ingredients and heat.

Place a little of the heated Sauce in the center of each plate with the pastry roll on top. Sprinkle with fresh cilantro and serve with fried rice.

Mushroom Crusted Chicken Smothered with Love

This is another favorite with men. I often make it without the mushroom crust and it works just as well.

2 Cornish hens or one 3–4lb/1½–2kg chicken, spatchcocked

To spatchcock, use a sharp knife to cut down the back of the chicken and flatten it as much as possible.

Marinade

¼ cup orange juice

¼ cup mango juice

1 cup honey

¼ cup soy sauce

¼ cup lemon juice

minced garlic to taste

1 tablespoon minced fresh ginger

Combine the Marinade ingredients in a dish large enough to hold the chickens. Place chickens in Marinade and marinate for 2–3 hours. Preheat oven to 350F/180C. Place chickens breast side up in an ovenproof baking dish with 1½ cups of the Marinade. Bake for about 1½ hours, basting every so often with the pan juices.

Simmer the remaining marinade on the stove until it reduces slightly.

Mushroom Crust

3 tablespoons oil

1 onion, finely chopped

2 cups black mushrooms, finely chopped

minced garlic, salt, black pepper
   and thyme to taste

Heat oil. Cook onion with garlic until onion is glossy.
Add mushrooms and seasonings and continue cooking
until heated through.

Remove the chickens from the oven and turn breast side
down. Cover with the mushroom crust, patting it firmly
in place. Brown the crusted chickens slightly under the
broiler. Serve by placing some chicken on each plate and
drizzling the Sauce over and around it. This is delicious
with Woo Me With Wild Rice Stir Fry (recipe page 62).

Heaven Sent
Singaporean

African Curry

Serves 6–8

I discovered this recipe in Singapore. The woman who taught it to me could not speak a word of English, so I had to figure it out making use of my senses of taste and smell. When I returned home, this was the first dish I made for Hamburger to show him how well I had spent his money. Boy, did this impress him and every man I have served it to since!

9–12 chicken thighs

1 small can tomato paste

½ cup plain yogurt (optional)

Marinate the chicken for a few hours with tomato paste spread over both sides. Adding yogurt to the tomato paste gives an extra flavor & makes the chicken even more tender.

3–4 tablespoons oil

1 cinnamon stick

1 star anise

5 coriander seeds

3 cloves

3 onions, chopped

minced garlic to taste

2 tablespoons fresh minced ginger

18oz/500g can chopped or sieved tomatoes

1 tablespoon brown sugar

1 teaspoon salt

pepper to taste

oil for deep-frying

4 potatoes, cubed
    and deep-fried for 10 minutes

Heat about 3–4 tablespoons oil in a pot large enough to fit all the chicken pieces. Add the Curry Paste and cook for a few minutes for the flavors to expel, adding more oil if necessary. Add cinnamon stick, star anise, coriander seeds and cloves. Toss. Add onions, garlic and ginger, and cook until onions are glossy. Add chicken pieces and cook for about 5–10 minutes. Add tomatoes, brown sugar, salt and pepper. Simmer for 45 minutes. Add potatoes and simmer for a further 30 minutes. Deep-frying the potatoes first prevents them from breaking in the curry. Serve over rice or couscous along with Yogurt and Cilantro Sauce.

Curry Paste

½ cup turmeric

1 tablespoon chili powder (use less if milder curry required)

1 tablespoon paprika

Mix the above with cold water to make a paste.

Yogurt and Cilantro Sauce

This Yogurt and Cilantro Sauce is delicious with all curries.

1 cup yogurt

3 tablespoons chopped cilantro

2 tablespoons finely chopped onion

2 tablespoons finely chopped tomato

2 tablespoons finely chopped cucumber

salt to taste

1 dry or fresh chili (optional)

Mix all the ingredients together. Serve as side dish with curries. Add 1–2 tablespoons fresh chopped mint when serving with lamb curry.

Baby, Baby Chickens
Piri-Piri

Nothing like a good, spicy hot piri-piri chicken to steal a man's heart!

2 Cornish hens or one 3–4lb/1½–2kg chicken, spatchcocked (cut down the back and opened as flat as possible)

coarse salt

black pepper

dried chili flakes

fresh lemon juice

minced garlic (optional)

poultry seasoning
    or spice for Portuguese chicken, if available

barbecue seasoning

Season both sides of the chicken well, splashing with lemon juice first. Allow to stand for a few hours or overnight.

Preheat the oven to 350F/180C. Roast breast side up for about an hour or until crispy. Use pan juices to baste continuously, or if using Piri-Piri Basting Sauce, mix with pan juices. If grilled on a barbecue for a few minutes after roasting, these chickens are even more fabulous!

Piri-Piri Basting Sauce

3 tablespoons butter

2 tablespoons piri-piri oil

minced garlic to taste

juice of 1–2 lemons

salt, chili paste or minced chilies, cayenne pepper to taste

Heat all ingredients in a saucepan until the butter has melted. Baste with this sauce every now and then while the chickens are cooking. Pour a little sauce over them just before serving and leave enough to serve on the side with the chickens. I often use this sauce over grilled fish – delicious!

Chapter Seven

Put Fire In His Loins

Even though these days red meat is considered by some to be unhealthy, there is nothing like a marvelous meat dish to overwhelm your man completely. If you are looking for total conquest, any of the following recipes will enslave him.

Beef with Raunchy

Serves 4–6

I adore Roquefort cheese & decided to add it to a pepper sauce to serve over beef, but if you prefer, you can leave out the cheese.

4–6 steaks of your choice,
  plus 1 small piece of steak for the sauce

1 tablespoon butter

1 tablespoon oil

2 tablespoons brandy

1 tablespoon green peppercorns, rinsed and
  crushed

½ cup Roquefort cheese, crumbled

1 cup cream

salt, black pepper and white pepper to taste

a few drops of Tabasco sauce

parsley and pink peppercorns for garnish

Heat oil and butter in a saucepan. Cook the small piece of steak until well done. Remove. Add the brandy and after a minute add the green peppercorns, which have been crushed with the back of a spoon or a mortar and pestle. Reduce the heat and add the cheese, cream, spices and Tabasco sauce. Gently whisk the sauce until it is smooth. Adjust seasonings. If Roquefort cheese is omitted, allow the sauce to simmer until reduced slightly.

Rub the steaks with a little oil. Season with salt and freshly ground black pepper just before cooking.
Heat a cast iron frying pan or cook steaks on a barbecue or under the broiler. I love eating these steaks with lots of coarsely ground black pepper pressed into the meat. Cook until desired doneness. Spoon the sauce over the steaks. Garnish with parsley and a sprinkling of pink peppercorns.

I sometimes make little "hats" to garnish these steaks. Fry small batches of cooked egg noodles in a little oil until golden brown on both sides. Place on top of steaks when ready to serve with 2 chives or the green part of scallions stuck into the noodles to resemble ears.

Roquefort Pepper Sauce

I was living in California after I divorced my first husband, Tabasco, and we had not seen each other for a few months. The day I returned to South Africa, we met at his house and his effect on me was as devastating as ever. We took one look at each other and burst out laughing, knowing we were about to fall into bed together. This was the dish I cooked in honor of our "reunion."

Sosaties from Africa with Love

Serves 4–6
This is a typical Cape Malay dish and is also delicious with lamb or chicken. It is a hot favorite with South African men.

1lb2oz/500g beef sirloin or lamb

Soak kebab sticks in water for about 30 minutes. Cut meat into cubes and thread onto kebab sticks with pieces of onion and different colored peppers in between.

Marinade

½ cup white vinegar

2 teaspoons curry powder

2 tablespoons brown sugar

2 tablespoons smooth apricot jam

3–4 bay leaves

salt to taste

Boil the above ingredients together until the sugar has dissolved and the mixture is smooth. Cool and pour over meat. Cover and place in fridge and allow to marinate for a few hours or overnight. Barbecue and baste with marinade during cooking. Serve with Romantic Basmati Rice with Toasted Cashews.

A Romantic Basmati Rice with Toasted Cashews

Better Than Chocolate added his magic touch to this dish by including vegetables and seafood and turning it into a paella.

2 cups Basmati rice

3 tablespoons butter plus 5–6 tablespoons oil

½ cup onions, sliced into ¼" rings

¼ teaspoon minced garlic

1 tablespoon sugar

1 teaspoon turmeric

1 cinnamon stick

2 cups water

salt and pepper

1 cup toasted cashew nuts

cilantro or parsley for garnish

Rinse rice well. Heat 1 tablespoon butter & 2 tablespoons oil in a heavy saucepan and brown rice for a few minutes. In a separate pan, heat 2 tablespoons of butter and 3 tablespoons of oil and cook onions and garlic. Sprinkle 1 tablespoon of sugar over the mixture and toss till the onions have caramelized slightly. Add to the rice. Add turmeric, cinnamon stick, water and seasonings. Bring to a boil and then reduce heat and simmer with the lid on until the rice is cooked (approximately 20–25 minutes). Remove cinnamon stick and adjust seasonings. Scatter with toasted cashews and chopped cilantro or parsley.

If adding other vegetables such as julienne strips of carrots, zucchini, arugula, and seafood or chicken, do so while cooking the onion. Omit the cashews and cinnamon stick.

Besame Mucho Osso Bucco with Gremolata

Serves 6–8

The traditional way of serving Osso Bucco is with gremolata, a combination of fresh parsley, anchovies and lemon zest, sprinkled on top. However, I could not resist putting the gremolata right into the Osso Bucco.

8–10 veal knuckles or shanks

3–4 tablespoons olive oil and 1–2 tablespoons butter

1 onion, chopped

3–4 anchovy fillets

salt, pepper and flour to dust veal

¼ cup white wine

2 cups chicken stock

2 tablespoons tomato paste

1 tablespoon brown sugar

1 tablespoon lemon zest

½ cup freshly chopped parley

Preheat oven to 350F/180C. Heat the oil and butter in a large pot. Cook onion until glossy. Add the anchovy fillets and cook till mushy. Dust the veal with salt, pepper and flour. Brown the veal and then add the wine and allow it to sizzle for a few minutes. Remove the veal to a casserole dish. Add the rest of ingredients to the pan juices and heat through. Pour this sauce over the veal and bake covered for 1½ hours or until tender. Correct seasonings and serve.

Osso Bucco is traditionally served with saffron risotto, but couscous or mashed potatoes are delicious as well. Chicken may be substituted for veal.

Linger Awhile Lamb Casserole

Serves 6–8
The advantage of this recipe is that you only use one casserole dish. This is wonderful to make on a cold winter's day. The aroma fills the house with the comforting promise of a special meal. Chicken may be substituted for lamb.

3lb/1½ kg stewing lamb, trimmed of fat

4 tablespoons oil for cooking

1½ tablespoons sugar

2 tablespoons flour

3 sweet potatoes, peeled and diced

3 large carrots, sliced into rounds

6–8 small new potatoes

2 onions, quartered

1 cup string beans

1 cup frozen corn

1 cup frozen petit pois peas

4 cups beef stock

2 tablespoons tomato paste

2 teaspoons dried rosemary or 3 fresh sprigs

1 sachet bouquet garni

salt, pepper and cayenne pepper to taste

Preheat oven to 350F/180C. Heat oil in frying pan. Add lamb and brown. Remove lamb, drain frying pan of excess oil and return lamb. Sprinkle with sugar and toss until sugar caramelizes. Sprinkle flour over meat and heat through.

Place lamb in a large casserole dish along with the rest of the ingredients. Cover and bake for 1½ hours, turning occasionally. Uncover and bake for a further 20 minutes. Remove bouquet garni, adjust seasonings and serve with couscous and chutney. If you can wait, it's even better served the next day.

$\mathcal{L}$ove Nest Lamb on Potato Straws

My second husband Icicle was passionate about lamb. These recipes turned out so well (far better than he did!) and I still eat them with gusto. This one is utterly superb.

Sauce

1 tablespoon oyster sauce

1 tablespoon soy sauce

1 tablespoon cornstarch
  mixed to a paste with a little water

2 teaspoons honey

1 teaspoon sugar

¼ –½ cup water

salt, black pepper & cayenne pepper to taste

Mix all the Sauce ingredients in a bowl and set aside.

2 tablespoons oil

minced garlic to taste

1–2 chilies, seeded and chopped

2 cups lamb loin, sliced

2 onions, chopped

2 red peppers, seeded and sliced

2 carrots, thinly sliced and steamed

1 cup baby corn, steamed

1 cup sugar snap peas or snow peas

3 tablespoons chopped fresh cilantro
  and/or mint for garnish

Heat oil in a frying pan or wok. Add garlic, chilies and lamb and cook till tender. Remove lamb from pan and cook onions till glossy, adding more oil if necessary. Add peppers, carrots, corn and peas. Toss till heated through. Add lamb and Sauce and heat until Sauce thickens slightly. Place a potato straw on each plate and pile some of the lamb mixture on top. Garnish with chopped cilantro and/or mint.

Potato Straws

4 potatoes, peeled or unpeeled,
   and grated

oil for frying

Place grated potatoes in lettuce spinner and dry well.
Heat oil in a frying pan & either make individual servings,
by using enough grated potatoes to cover a saucer, or use
all the potatoes to make one large one. Make sure that
the potatoes are distributed evenly. Once the first side
is golden brown, turn over and cook the other side until
crispy. Drain on paper towels.

Lip-Smacking Lamb

There is nothing in the world to beat a good lamb dish and it's the fastest and most efficient way to a man's heart. My second mother-in-law made the best roast lamb I have ever tasted. Since I hate to fall short in any cooking competition, whether real or imagined, I set out to improve on it, but there was really not much to improve.

I find that the lamb shoulder is more tender than the leg. I also trim off most of the fat.

shoulder of lamb

salt, white pepper and Aromat or Accent

2 onions, quartered

2 cups of water

1 tablespoon good quality beef gravy powder

Place the lamb in a roasting pan and season well with salt, pepper and Aromat or Accent. Place the onions around it and add the two cups of water. Cover and roast for 3 hours in a 350F/180C oven. Uncover for the last half hour. Pour the juices into a saucepan, removing as much fat as possible. Add the gravy powder and heat till thickened.

There is nothing like this lamb served with crispy roast potatoes, sautéed string beans and Caramelized Butternut Squash (recipe page 49). I can honestly say that I have yet to serve this to a man who hasn't fallen in love with me.

Love Me or

Leave Me Veal with Couscous

This is the most sensational veal dish I know. The response whenever I serve it is always the same – total satisfaction!

8 pieces of veal scaloppine – or slices of veal that have been pounded quite thin

salt, pepper and flour to dust veal

3 tablespoons butter

3 tablespoons oil

¼ cup Calvados

1 tablespoon flour

1½ cups chicken stock

¼ cup white wine

2 tablespoons sherry

2 tablespoons butter + 2 tablespoons oil

6 zucchini cut into fairly thin rings

crushed clove of garlic

2 cups mushrooms

2 cups Neapolitane Sauce (recipe page 69)

8 slices of Emmenthaler or Gruyère cheese

Season veal with salt and pepper and coat with flour. Heat the butter and oil in a pan. Sauté the veal on both sides. Splash with Calvados and allow to sizzle for a few minutes. Remove the veal from the pan and set aside. Take the pan off the heat and stir in the flour. Put the pan back on the burner and add the chicken stock, wine and sherry. Simmer for a few minutes. Replace the veal in the pan and simmer for 5 minutes. Set aside.

In another saucepan heat 2 tablespoons butter with 2 tablespoons oil and sauté the zucchini, garlic and mushrooms. Add the Neapolitane Sauce. Season with salt and pepper. At the bottom of a casserole dish place the zucchini and Neapolitane Sauce. Remove the veal slices from the gravy and place on top. Top each slice of veal with a slice of cheese and then pour the gravy over the cheese. Bake in a preheated 350F/180C oven for 20–30 minutes. Serve with couscous.

Make the Love Rise

Breads

There isn't a man on earth who isn't impressed with a woman who makes her own bread.
Accept that he will be around for life, because once he has sunk his teeth
into any of these breads you will never be able to get rid of him!

Love Bite Bagels

Yields 10–12

People often ask me why I don't get fat when I'm always in the kitchen. The reason is that I eat about three of these bagels a day. It's not the bread that's fattening, it's what you put on it. These are so good that adding butter or anything else is completely unnecessary.

6 cups cake flour
  (using bread flour will make a heavier bagel)

2¼ teaspoons fast rising instant yeast
  (2 packets) or ¼oz/7g active dry yeast

½ cup sugar

1 tablespoon salt

½ cup oil

2 eggs, beaten

2 cups warm water

Place dry ingredients in a mixing bowl. Make a well in the center and add liquids. Knead well. The dough must not be sticky. Brush the top of the ball of dough with a little oil to keep it from drying out. Cover with plastic wrap and a dishtowel and allow to rise in a draft free area until doubled in bulk. Punch down. Break off pieces of dough (slightly smaller than the size of a tennis ball) and roll into a sausage shape. Circle the dough around your hand and pinch the edges together so that they are secure. The dough should yield 10 to 12 bagels.

Place on a greased baking sheet or directly on an oven rack that has been removed from the oven and covered with greased tin foil. I prefer using the oven rack covered with foil as all the bagels can fit on it. Allow to rise 30 minutes.

Preheat oven to 350F/180C. Heat a large pot of water on the stove and, when boiling, add three bagels at a time. Cover and allow to simmer for about 1–2 minutes. Turn the bagels over and repeat. Place bagels back on foil-covered oven rack. Poppy seeds or sesame seeds may be sprinkled on top at this stage. Bake for about 30 minutes or until golden brown. After 20 minutes, turn the bagels over so that they bake evenly.

My mother makes the best whole-wheat bagels I have ever tasted. Use 4 cups cake flour and 2 cups whole wheat flour. One tablespoon of caraway seeds added to the flour gives a terrific flavor. The rest of the ingredients remain the same.

Foxy Focaccia with Herbs, Cheese and

Serves 6–8
This is one of my favorite recipes and I use this dough as a basis for a variety of breads. It is simple to make and never fails.

Basic Focaccia

3 cups all-purpose flour

1 package fast rising instant yeast

1 teaspoon salt

1 teaspoon sugar

1 tablespoon oil

1½ cups warm water

Place dry ingredients in a mixing bowl. Make a well in the center and add liquids. Knead well until dough is elastic. Brush top of dough with oil, cover with plastic wrap and a dishtowel. Place in a draft free area and allow to rise until doubled in bulk. Punch down. Preheat oven to 350F/180C.

Shape dough into an oval and place on a greased baking sheet, patting the dough down until it is fairly flat. Brush with melted butter and sprinkle seasonings of your choice, such as coarse or ordinary salt, fresh rosemary dipped in oil, oregano or thyme. Pitted olives cut in half, tomato slices, fried onions or sun-dried tomatoes may also be placed on top of the dough. Bake for about 30 minutes or until golden brown. This bread freezes well, but always heat it till crispy before serving.

Serve bread with some olive oil and a dash of balsamic vinegar to dip into. Olive Paste is also delicious.

Olive Paste

1 cup pitted black olives

½ cup green stuffed olives

1–2 tablespoons each, oil, vinegar and sugar to taste

Blend in food processor till fairly smooth.

Herbed Focaccia

Use the Basic Focaccia recipe but after you punch the dough down, roll it into a rectangle. Brush with melted butter and sprinkle with a variety of herbs, such as Italian herbs, oregano, salt, black pepper. Fold dough over, shape into a crescent and make a few 1"/3cm slits through the outside edges of the crescent. Brush the top with more melted butter and sprinkle with more herbs. Bake in a preheated 350F/180C oven for 30 minutes or until golden brown.

Cheese Focaccia

Use the Basic Focaccia recipe but after you punch the dough down, roll it into a rectangle. Sprinkle with 2 cups of grated mozzarella cheese. Fold the dough over, shape into a crescent, brush with melted butter and sprinkle with salt and a combination of herbs such as oregano, basil, Italian herbs, rosemary. Bake in a preheated 350F/180C oven for 30 minutes or until golden brown.

Who Loves You? Whole Wheat Bread

After I divorced my children's father, I was determined to envelop them in a warm and loving atmosphere.

I thought that the best way to achieve this was for them to grow up in a home where the aroma of fresh bread perfumed the air. I took great pride in presenting them with my latest concoctions. I am totally convinced that my breads have a magical effect, because my sons have grown up without any of my dysfunctions!

Yields 3 loaves
I have devoted much of my cooking time to perfecting
my bread recipes, which are a staple of my diet. For years
I battled to make whole wheat bread that didn't crumble
and toasted well. This is what I finally came up with.

Yogurt Seeded Loaf

8 cups whole wheat flour

2 cups All Bran flakes

2 cups cracked wheat or bulgur wheat

2 tablespoons flax seeds

2 tablespoons sunflower seeds

2 tablespoons sesame seeds

2 teaspoons baking powder

1 tablespoon salt

2 teaspoons baking soda

4 cups yogurt

2 cups water

½ cup honey plus 3 tablespoons brown sugar

2 teaspoons oil

Preheat the oven to 350F/180C. Mix dry ingredients.
Add yogurt, water, honey and oil. Mix to a sloppy
consistency. Grease 3 bread tins and fill with dough,
making sure the dough is packed tightly in the tin. Scatter
the tops with a combination of flax, sunflower, pumpkin,
poppy and sesame seeds. Wet the back of a spoon and
gently press the seeds into the surface of the dough. Bake
for 1 hour. Freezes well.

Yeast Loaf

6 cups all-purpose flour

2 cups whole wheat flour

1 cup cracked wheat or bulgur

1 cup bran

3 packages fast rising instant yeast

1 tablespoon salt

4 cups warm water

¾ cup oil

½ cup corn syrup

sunflower, poppy, sesame
    and pumpkin seeds for sprinkling

Mix dry ingredients. Make a well in the center and add
liquids. Knead well, until dough is elastic. Divide dough
into three bread tins, sprinkle with a combination of
sunflower, poppy, sesame and pumpkin seeds. Gently
press the seeds into the surface of the dough using the
back of a wet spoon. Cover with a dishtowel and allow
to rise until the dough reaches the top of the tins. Preheat
oven to 350F/180C. Bake for about 45 minutes or until
golden brown.

Holiday with Challah

Yields 2 loaves

Waking up in the morning to fried eggs and homemade Challah toast is a treat to tantalize your taste buds.

9 cups all-purpose flour

3 packages fast rising instant yeast

¾ cup sugar

1 rounded tablespoon salt

2 eggs, beaten

½ cup oil

3 cups warm water

poppy and sesame seeds for sprinkling
    and an extra beaten egg

Place all the dry ingredients in a large mixing bowl. Make a well in the center and add the liquids. Knead well and form a ball. Brush with a little oil to prevent the dough from drying out. Cover with plastic wrap (I often use a plastic shopping bag) and a dishtowel. Place in a draft free area (in an oven or microwave) and allow to rise until doubled in bulk.

Punch down and roll the dough loosely into a long thick sausage. Divide in half and divide one of the halves into three equal pieces. Roll each piece into a long sausage, pinch the ends of the three pieces together, tucking the end gently underneath, and braid the three strands. Secure the end in the same way. Repeat with the other half of the dough and place both on a greased baking sheet. Brush with the beaten egg and sprinkle one loaf with poppy seeds and the other with sesame seeds. Allow the loaves to sit for 30 minutes.

Preheat the oven to 350F/180C and place a dish of water in the bottom of the oven. This will give the bread a wonderful crispy crust. Bake for 45 minutes or until golden brown.

Another method for forming the loaves is to divide each half of the dough into 2 pieces, not 3. Roll each piece into a long, thickish sausage. Pinch the two ends together and wind the two pieces of dough around each other, twisting as you do so. Pinch the ends together, form into a circle and close by pinching both ends of the dough together. Repeat with the other half of the dough.

Sultry Saffron Bread with Couscous & Vegetables

Serves 6–8

A good piece of homemade bread can spin a man into anything you want him to be. Served with a salad, this is a meal on its own. It's also a great recipe if you want to impress guests.

1 teaspoon saffron threads

½ cup boiling water

3 cups all-purpose flour

1 package fast rising instant yeast

2 teaspoons salt

2 teaspoons sugar

1 tablespoon oil

1 cup warm water

1 cup hot chicken stock

½ cup couscous

1 eggplant, thinly sliced lengthwise

1 onion, chopped

2 red peppers, cut in half and seeded

3 tablespoons oil

1 cup canned small beans

4 tablespoons chopped cilantro or parsley

Stir saffron threads into the boiling water and leave to cool. Place flour, yeast, salt and sugar into a mixing bowl. Stir in dissolved saffron threads. Add 1 tablespoon oil and 1 cup warm water. Knead. Cover with plastic wrap and a dishtowel and allow to rise until doubled in bulk.

Pour hot stock over couscous and leave to stand. Fluff after a little while and add some boiling water if not yet puffed and soft. Mix through.

Sprinkle eggplant with salt and allow to sit for 30 minutes. Rinse well. Place eggplant, onion and red peppers on a baking sheet, drizzle with 3 tablespoons oil, sprinkle with salt and pepper and grill until lightly browned.

Punch dough down and roll into a rectangle. Brush with a little melted butter. Place the eggplant across half the length of the dough, top with the couscous, red peppers and beans and onions. Fold dough over and pinch the edges closed, using water if necessary. Brush with egg wash or melted butter and sprinkle with salt and cilantro or parsley. Bake in a preheated 350F/180C oven for about 30 minutes or until golden brown.

I Love You, I Want You Walnut Bread

Yields 2 loaves

Tabasco once took me on a skiing trip to Club Med in Colorado. They served a walnut bread that I couldn't get enough of. This is my version. It's fabulous to toast and great for sandwiches as well.

6 cups all-purpose flour

2 packages active dry yeast

¼ cup sugar

1 tablespoon salt

1½ cups coarsely chopped walnuts

½ cup oil

3 cups warm water

Mix dry ingredients, including the nuts. Make a well in the center and add liquids. Knead well until dough is elastic. Divide mixture in half and place in two greased bread tins. Cover with a dishtowel and allow to rise until the dough touches the top of the tins. Bake in a preheated 350F/180C oven for 40 minutes or until golden brown.

Sandwiches are Sexy!

Every boyfriend (and husband) I have had gets euphoric when they talk about the sandwiches I make. Forget about sexy lingerie, dim lights and scented oils – these sandwiches hit the spot quicker and more effectively than any words whispered in his ear.

Use any bread of your choice and fill with an assortment of Roasted Vegetables (recipe page 48). My favorites are egg-plants, zucchini and sun-dried tomatoes. I often put slices of mozzarella or robbiola (a fresh Italian cow's milk cheese) on top and drizzle a little Pesto (recipe page 69) over it.

You can also use a combination of different rolls or breads. Substitute Homemade Mayonnaise (recipe page 41) for butter. Place a variety of lettuce greens on the bread or roll, and layer any of your favorite fillings, such as spicy cajun chicken breasts, a thick layer of sprouts, a drizzle of any of my Vinaigrette Dressings (recipes page 40), a slice of cheese, sliced tomatoes, pommery or hot mustard, and finally, top with another slice of bread or roll to close the sandwich.

If making a meat sandwich, add some piccalilli. Brisket with horseradish is also an idea. Make a kebab out of pickled onions, cherry tomatoes and radishes placed on a toothpick and stick it on top of the sandwich, or use a pickle. Slice through the length to the base a few times, fan it out and anchor it with a toothpick. Garnish the plate with endive lettuce, lemon twists, watercress and cherry tomatoes. Serve with French fries (French fries made from sweet potatoes are delicious). You may also choose to toast the inside of the bread or roll.

Another idea is to make a round Challah – the version on page 134 that's twisted into a circle. Slice it in half through the middle, spread Homemade Mayonnaise on both sides and add a layer of lettuce. Then fill small sections with different fillings, for example, roasted vegetables in one section, then smoked salmon and cream cheese; egg salad with red peppers and chili paste; smoked chicken, tuna and olives. Use your imagination to make it as interesting and colorful as possible.

Use Pickled Cucumbers and Pickled Peppers (recipes page 58) to garnish all these sandwiches.

Marinated Chicken with Toasted Focaccia Fantastico

6 boneless chicken breasts

½ cup soy sauce

3 tablespoons sherry

1 teaspoon minced ginger

minced garlic to taste

Homemade Mayonnaise (recipe page 41)

6 slices Focaccia, toasted (recipe page 131)

arugula or watercress

1 cup cherry tomatoes

sun-dried tomatoes

½ cup toasted pine nuts

robbiola cheese (optional)

parsley or watercress for garnish

Marinate chicken in soy sauce, sherry, ginger and garlic for a few hours. Grill the chicken or brown in a pan, using a small amount of oil or cooking spray. Spread Homemade Mayonnaise on toasted Focaccia, using two pieces per person and serving as an open sandwich. Layer arugula or watercress on top of Mayonnaise, and then the chicken. Sauté cherry tomatoes in a little oil sprinkled with salt. Add to the sandwich along with sun-dried tomatoes and toasted pine nuts. Serve with a slice of robbiola cheese placed in the center of the plate, and garnish with chopped parsley and a sprig of watercress.

Pita sandwiches are at the top of my list of fun food. They are messy, delicious and satisfying. I serve them at informal parties, lunches, Sunday suppers, as picnic or bed food, and everything in between. Use any combination of ingredients with Tahini Sauce, and/or Turkish Salad as a spread.

> 1 package fresh pita bread
> – try and avoid the frozen ones
> Israeli Salad
> Turkish Salad
> Tahini Sauce
> choice of chicken, beef, lamb or Roasted
> Vegetables (recipe page 48)

Heat the pitas and cut them in half. Split open. Spread the Turkish Salad on the inside of the pita. Place a little Israeli Salad at the bottom of the pita, then a layer of meat or Roasted Vegetables, drizzle with Tahini Sauce, more Israeli Salad, a little more meat or Roasted Vegetables and another dollop of Tahini Sauce.

Israeli Salad

This is a traditional Israeli salad. Whenever I make pita pockets I include this salad as a filling.

> 3–4 tomatoes
> 1 red pepper and/or 1 yellow pepper
> 1 cucumber
> 4 scallions
> oil and vinegar, or lemon juice if preferred
> salt, black pepper, sugar to taste

Chop all the vegetables into very small pieces. Place in bowl and drizzle with oil and vinegar, using slightly more oil than vinegar or lemon juice. Season well.

Salad & Tahini Sauce)

Turkish Salad

This is another salad that is found in many of the restaurants and delis in Israel. It's great as a spread for sandwiches or to use as a condiment with roasts and fish.

> 3–4 tablespoons oil
> 1 onion, chopped
> minced garlic to taste
> 3 red peppers, chopped
> ½ cup water
> ½ cup tomato paste
> ½ cup chopped parsley
> salt, black pepper, brown sugar to taste
> ½ teaspoon chili paste or 1–2 fresh
>   or dried chilies

Heat oil in a saucepan. Cook onion and garlic until onion is glossy. Add peppers and toss for a few minutes. Add water, tomato paste, parsley and seasonings and allow to simmer until peppers are soft. Place in food processor and process till smooth. Adjust seasonings. It should be quite spicy. Allow to cool. Store in fridge. Serve at room temperature.

Tahini Sauce

> 1 cup tahini (sesame) paste
> 1 cup water
> juice of 2 lemons
> salt, pepper, paprika and minced garlic to taste
> 3 tablespoons chopped parsley

Place tahini paste and water in food processor. Add lemon juice along with the seasonings and parsley. Process until smooth. Check seasonings. It's important to get the correct balance of lemon juice, salt and garlic.

6 slices beef fillet or sirloin

1 cup barbecue sauce

1 tablespoon seeded mustard

1 tablespoon honey

1–2 dried or fresh chilies

sliced and toasted Walnut Bread
(recipe page 138)

Homemade Mayonnaise (recipe page 41)

lettuce, watercress or arugula

4 onions, sliced into rings and caramelized

Pickled Peppers (recipe page 58)

4 leeks, finely sliced and deep-fried

watercress and red peppers for garnish

Place barbecue sauce, mustard, honey and chilies in a mixing bowl. Add steak pieces and marinate for a few hours. This marinade is also wonderful as a sauce for a chicken stir-fry with baby corn, snow peas and pasta, served with cashew nuts.

Place a slice of toasted Walnut Bread on a plate, spread with Homemade Mayonnaise, top with chosen greens, Caramelized Onions, Pickled Peppers and steak. Cover with another piece of Walnut Bread. Pile deep-fried leeks on top. Garnish with watercress and chopped red peppers.

Caramelized Onions

2 tablespoons oil

4 onions, sliced into rings

1 tablespoons sugar

2 tablespoons balsamic vinegar

salt to taste

Heat oil. Add onions and cook until they just start to brown. Sprinkle with sugar and drizzle with vinegar and cook until onions are thoroughly browned and tender. These onions are fantastic with any sandwich or as an accompaniment to any meal.

Love, Lust & Laffa

This is a staple dish in Israeli delis. It satisfies the most ravenous of appetites.

The difference between a Laffa and a Pita Sandwich is that in a Laffa the pita bread is larger and thinner. Use a large, thin tortilla as an alternative if large pitas are not available. Fill with any of the Pita Sandwich filling suggestions, but top with French fries. Then roll up to form a cone shape, wrap in foil to prevent sauce from dripping, and watch his ecstatic reaction.

Feeling Peckish, Darling?

The ultimate sophisticated seduction is serving tea in a silver tea set
with an assortment of any of these cookies – presented on a silver platter, of course.
Or they're just fabulous to stuff into your mouth after a bout of wild,
passionate bedroom gymnastics!

Cha-cha Chocolate & Nuts

Yields 15

¾ cup all-purpose flour

1 tablespoon custard powder

2 tablespoons icing sugar

¼ cup butter

1 tablespoon water

7oz/200g sweetened milk chocolate for baking

1 box of nutty chocolates
   or any chocolate-covered nuts

Place flour, custard powder and icing sugar in a mixing bowl. Rub in the butter and add enough water for the mixture to cling together. Put in the fridge for about 30 minutes or in the freezer for 15 minutes. Break off spoon-size pieces of dough and press down with a fork onto a greased baking sheet. Preheat oven to 350F/180C and bake for about 15 minutes or until golden brown. Allow to cool on a wire rack.

Melt chocolate over hot water or in the microwave. Dip a piece of nutty chocolate into the melted chocolate and stick onto the cookie. Drizzle a little more chocolate over the nut to cover. Store in an airtight container when cooled.

Florentine Fantasies

Yields 15

½ cup butter

¼ cup sugar

1 tablespoon corn syrup

1 teaspoon lemon juice

1 cup chopped macadamia nuts

½ cup all-purpose flour

1 cup fruit & nut cake mix
or Harvest Medley of dried cranberries,
apples and cherries

7oz/200g sweetened milk chocolate for baking

Preheat oven to 350F/180C. Heat butter, sugar, syrup and lemon juice. Add nuts, flour and mixed fruit and nut cake mix or Harvest Medley. Grease a baking sheet. Place heaped teaspoonfuls of cookie dough on baking sheet, well separated. Flatten slightly with the back of a spoon. Bake for 10–15 minutes. Place on a wire rack to cool. As they cool, they harden. Melt chocolate over hot water or in the microwave, and spread over the bottom of each cookie. Allow to set. Store in an airtight container.

Goin' Nuts with Pecans & Walnuts

Yields 30

7oz/200g salted biscuits, saltines
   or any lightly salted cracker

4oz/100g walnuts, chopped

3 egg whites

1 cup sugar

2 teaspoons vanilla

pecans

melted sweetened milk chocolate for baking

Preheat oven to 350F/180C. Crush biscuits in food processor until fine. Put in a bowl and mix in nuts. Beat egg whites until stiff; gradually add sugar and vanilla. Fold egg whites into biscuit and nut mixture. Place in an 8" x 12"/20cm x 30cm ovenproof dish and bake for 30 minutes or until golden brown. Slice into squares, allow to cool and place on a wire rack. Using melted chocolate, stick a pecan nut on each cookie & pipe a little chocolate over the nut with a pastry bag.

Once More Orange Cookies with Chocolate & Almonds

Yields 15–20

He'll think you are so hot when you whip these up and serve them after a great meal. I often serve them along with Friandise, fruit dipped in caramelized sugar (recipe page 183). I can't think of a sweeter seduction!

¾ cup butter
½ cup icing/powdered sugar
finely grated rind of one orange
approximately 1½ cups all-purpose flour
½ cup self-raising flour
1 tablespoon cornstarch

Preheat oven to 350F/180C. Cream butter, icing sugar and orange rind until light and fluffy. Add flours and cornstarch and beat until smooth. Add more flour if the dough is not firm enough to handle. Form into small balls the size of a quarter. Place on a greased baking sheet and press down gently using the tines of a fork. Bake for about 10 minutes or until golden brown. Cool on wire racks.

Topping

¼ cup butter, softened
¾ cup icing sugar
1 cup flaked almonds
½ cup sweetened milk chocolate
    for baking, melted

Mix the butter and powdered sugar together until a good consistency is achieved. Add more powdered sugar if too sticky or more butter if too dry. Place in a pastry bag and using the star nozzle pipe a little onto the top of each biscuit. Drizzle the chocolate over the top. Scatter a few almonds on to the chocolate and allow to set.

Chapter Ten

Waking Up To Declarations of Love

Breakfast Bliss, Muffins & Sweet Buns

For me muffins and breakfast dishes have always conjured up thoughts of
Sunday mornings with a delicious lover, the sheets all tangled,
the newspapers scattered on the floor, and eating naked in bed.

Shameless Shukshuka

My nephew Bo is mad about eggs and this is his favorite breakfast. It's a typical Arabic dish but I make it with a slight Italian influence. Serve this with thickly buttered Challah toast or bagels.

3–4 tablespoons oil

1 onion, chopped

2 bay leaves

minced garlic to taste

1 x 16oz/450g can chopped tomatoes

1 cup sieved tomatoes

1 teaspoon oregano

salt, black pepper, cayenne pepper
    and brown sugar to taste

1 tablespoon Pesto (optional, recipe page 69)

4 eggs

Heat oil in pot. Add onion, bay leaves and garlic, and cook until onion is glossy. Add tomatoes, seasonings and Pesto and simmer for 30 minutes. Adjust seasonings. If too watery, add 1–2 tablespoons of tomato paste. Gently break the eggs into the sauce, cover and simmer until eggs are cooked through. Spoon a little of the sauce over the eggs as they are cooking. Ladle the sauce with the eggs into soup bowls. Serve with toasted Challah or bagels.

Come to Me Tomato Omelet

I love a well-made tomato omelet & refuse to compromise. It has to be perfect, like this recipe.

> 4 fresh tomatoes, skinned and chopped
>
> butter for cooking
>
> salt, black pepper and sugar to taste
>
> dried oregano
>
> 1 tablespoon tomato paste
>
> 2 eggs per person beaten
>   with 3–4 tablespoons milk

Skin the tomatoes by placing them in a bowl of boiling water for a few minutes. Then peel and chop. Heat 2 tablespoons butter in a saucepan. When it is sizzling, add the tomatoes with the seasonings and cook for a few minutes, covered, until the tomatoes are soft. Add tomato paste if mixture is too runny. Set aside.

Preheat the broiler in the oven. Heat about 2 tablespoons of butter in an omelet pan that can go in the oven. Add the beaten eggs. Using a fork, gently lift the sides of the omelet as it cooks, tilting the pan so that the egg runs under and can cook evenly. Spoon some of the cooked tomatoes onto the middle of the omelet and then place directly under the broiler for a minute or two. This will puff up the omelet. Fold the omelet over and slide onto a serving plate.

Variations

Sprinkle grated cheese over the tomato mixture or add sautéed mushrooms for variety. I often make Tomato Omelets with Neapolitane Sauce (recipe page 69), which is really sensational. It's also fantastic with a dollop of guacamole, salsa and sour cream on top.

French Toast for Lovers

This is rich and decadent and a wonderful way to end a passion-filled weekend.

8oz/250ml tub cream cheese

3–4 tablespoons sugar

2 tsp cinnamon

½ cup chopped pecans

6 small cocktail or hot-dog rolls

2 eggs beaten with a little milk and melted butter

Mix cream cheese with sugar and cinnamon. Add more sugar if necessary. Fold in pecans. Slice rolls in half and stuff with cream cheese mixture. Heat butter, dip the stuffed rolls in the beaten egg and fry until golden brown. Sprinkle with additional cinnamon and sugar and drizzle with honey or maple syrup if desired.

Mischievous Muffins

For some scientific reason that I do not understand, the cream cheese doesn't melt and remains in the center of these muffins. I am still impressed with my invention whenever I make them – and they taste superb.

2 cups all-purpose flour

1 cup whole wheat flour

4 teaspoons baking powder

1 teaspoon salt

2 teaspoons cinnamon

1¼ cups brown sugar

4 eggs

½ cup milk

½ cup oil

1½ cups cooked & puréed butternut squash

4oz/100g Philadelphia or Kiri cream cheese

Use Streusel Topping from Smooching Streusel Banana Muffins (recipe page 162).

Mix dry ingredients in a bowl. Add eggs and liquids. Add butternut purée. Half fill greased muffin tins with batter. Add a slice of cream cheese large enough to cover most of the batter and then spoon more batter over the cheese until the muffin cup is filled. Sprinkle with Streusel Topping. Bake in a preheated 350F/180C oven for 20–25 minutes.

with Butternut & Cream Cheese

Smooching Streusel

I went to my school graduation dance with Butterscotch because my boyfriend at the time, Oyster, had refused to attend. He didn't like the idea of me going with someone else, but I was determined. At the end of the evening, Butterscotch took me home and we were sitting in his car talking and flirting when he leaned over to kiss me. Just then a car drove up with Oyster's brother and friend inside. He had sent them to spy on us – and I guess with good reason! That put a swift end to the kiss and I got out of the car. We never recaptured that moment again. Until …

I ran into Butterscotch 20 years later and we went for a drink. He was more gorgeous than ever. After the first apple martini, I was brave enough to tell him that I had been mad about him at school. He confessed that he'd thought his teenage crush on me was unreciprocated. At the end of the evening, we found ourselves sitting in the car again, but this time the kiss was delivered – and it had 20 years of passion behind it! It was certainly worth the wait. The next evening, he came over for coffee where I served these muffins and we picked up where we had left off.

Banana Muffins

Yields 12

Every time I think of bananas or muffins, my heart catches in my throat, my pulse races, my face flushes and my lips turn up into a huge smile. I hope these muffins have the same effect on you.

3 cups all-purpose flour

4 teaspoons baking powder

pinch of salt

1 cup brown sugar

1 tablespoon ground ginger

4 eggs

½ cup oil

½ cup milk

3 bananas, chopped

Place dry ingredients in a bowl. Add eggs and liquids and fold in bananas. Spoon into greased muffin tins, sprinkle with Streusel Topping & bake in a preheated 350F/180C oven for 25 minutes.

Streusel Topping

1 cup all-purpose flour

4 tablespoons brown sugar

⅓ cup coconut

¾ cup chopped pecans

3 tablespoons melted butter

Place all ingredients in bowl and mix until crumbly.

Capricious Carrot Muffins

3 cups all-purpose flour

4 teaspoons baking powder

1½ cups brown sugar

3 teaspoons cinnamon

1 teaspoon salt

4 eggs

½ cup oil

½ cup milk

2 teaspoons vanilla extract

2 cups grated carrots

½ cup chopped pecans

Maple Cream Cheese Topping

4 cups icing sugar

½ cup cream cheese

1 tablespoon maple syrup

1 tablespoon butter

Place dry ingredients in a bowl. Add eggs and liquids. Fold in carrots and nuts. Spoon into greased muffin tins and bake in a preheated 350F/180C oven for 25 minutes. Allow to cool and then spread Maple Cream Cheese on top. Sprinkle some grated carrot over them and they'll look fabulous.

Place all the ingredients in a food processor and blend until smooth.

The Scone Seduction

The most romantic treat you can serve for tea are these scones with lashings of whipped cream, strawberry jam and fresh, succulent, juicy strawberries. This makes the ritual of tea a truly sensational experience.

2 cups all-purpose flour

4 teaspoons baking powder

1 tablespoon sugar

pinch of salt

4 tablespoons butter

3 teaspoons vanilla extract

1 egg beaten in an 8oz/250g measuring cup and then filled to the top with milk

Preheat oven to 350F/180C. Place dry ingredients in a mixing bowl. Add the butter and rub together using fingertips. Add liquids and mix well. Grease muffin tins and spoon in enough mixture to reach the rim of each cup. Bake for 25 minutes or until lightly golden brown. Allow to cool. Split open and top each half with strawberry jam, fresh strawberries and whipped cream.

Blissful Boolkas,

There is nothing in the world to touch a good Boolka (sweet milk bun). They are sustenance for the soul, nourishment for the heart and pure bliss for the taste buds. Any man waking up to Boolkas baking in the oven, with the aroma of cinnamon perfuming the air, will definitely not leave before breakfast!

Babkes and Hammentassen

When my grandmother lived with us, she would wake me up every morning for school with a cup of creamy coffee and a hot Boolka. Whenever I make Boolkas, I sit in bed dunking them in my coffee and cherishing every bite.

Boolkas

Yields about 40

8 cups all-purpose flour

3 packages fast rising instant yeast

1 tablespoon baking powder

1 cup sugar

1 teaspoon salt

1 cup butter

3 tablespoons oil

2 ⅓ cups milk

4 eggs, separated

melted butter

brown or white sugar

cinnamon

beaten egg

To make Boolkas, place dry ingredients in a mixing bowl. Melt butter and add oil and milk to it. Separate eggs, beat egg yolks and add to milk and butter mixture. The mixture must be lukewarm. Beat egg whites till stiff. Add liquids to dry ingredients and mix. Gently fold the whites into the mixture a little at a time. Use a large spoon to mix and not your hands. The less you handle the dough, the lighter the texture. The dough should be sticky so do not add more flour. Cover with a dishtowel and allow to rise in a draft free area until doubled in bulk.

Gently punch dough down, roll loosely into a fat sausage and divide in half. Lightly flour a work area. Roll each piece of dough into a rectangle. Brush with melted butter and sprinkle generously with brown or white sugar and cinnamon. Roll up, from end to end. Slice into 1"/2cm pieces and lay cut side down on a greased baking sheet. (I cover the rack of the oven with greased foil so that they will all fit on.) Brush with beaten egg and sprinkle with Farfel Topping.

Preheat oven to 350F/180C. Allow Boolkas to rise for another 30 minutes. Place in oven and bake for 30 minutes or until golden brown.

Farfel Topping

2 tablespoons butter

4 tablespoons all-purpose flour

4 tablespoons granulated sugar

Melt butter in a saucepan. Add flour and sugar and continue adding equal quantities of flour and sugar until the mixture becomes dry and crumbly.

Babke

A Babke is similar to a Boolka but it is shaped into a crescent. The same dough is used to make Hammentassens, which may be filled with poppy seeds or cream cheese. If ever you have the need to make a man fall instantly in love with you, serve him one of these and watch the magic cast its spell.

The other half of the Boolka dough may be made into a Babke. Roll it out into a rectangle, brush with melted butter and generously sprinkle with sugar and cinnamon. Fold one side lengthwise to the middle of the dough and then cover with the other side. Gently lift and place on a greased baking sheet or oven rack covered with greased foil. Shape it into a crescent. Make 1¼"/3cm slits on the outside edges of the Babke. Brush with beaten egg and sprinkle with Farfel Topping. Allow to rise for 30 minutes and then bake in a preheated 350F/180C oven for 30 minutes, or until golden brown.

Hammentassen

Yields about 40
I often use half the dough for Boolkas and half for Hammentassen. If using all the dough for Hammentassen, double the cheese mixture.

Cheese Filling

3 x 8oz/250ml tubs cream cheese

3–4 tablespoons granulated sugar

1 tablespoon cinnamon

 beaten egg

Mix ingredients together. It should be very sweet with a strong cinnamon flavor. Roll half the dough out into a rectangle. Cut into squares measuring 4"/10cm. Place a tablespoon of Cheese Filling in the center of each square. Pinch opposite edges together. Brush with beaten egg and sprinkle with Farfel Topping. They can also be made by cutting the dough into circles. Slash one side midway and fold the dough in a crisscross fashion to form a crescent shape.

Chapter Eleven

Ultimate Temptations

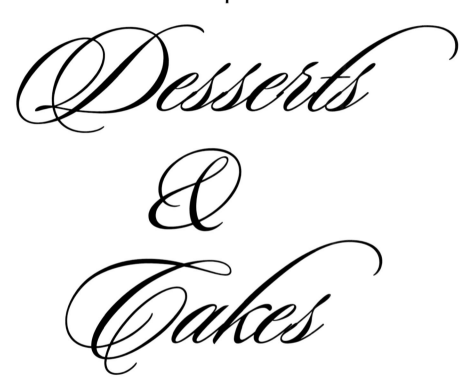

Desserts & Cakes

For some reason, men look at desserts the same sensuous way they look at an attractive woman.
So, if you wish to cultivate this look in your man, any of these desserts is guaranteed to do the trick.
They are as seductive to women as they are to men, except that women respond
in a far more intelligent way – with a loud "Oooh" and a sigh!

Hot 'n' Bothered Bananas

Serves 8
One bite of these and men go ga-ga!

4-6 bananas
self-raising flour
water
oil for deep frying
maple syrup
sesame seeds

Make a mixture of the self-raising flour and water that is not too thick or too thin, but will coat the bananas. Slice the bananas into ¾"/2cm pieces and dip into flour mixture. Heat oil in frying pan – about 1"/2–3cm deep – and fry bananas until they are puffed and golden brown. Drain on paper towels. Place on individual plates, drizzle with maple syrup and sprinkle with sesame seeds. Piping Chinese symbols in apricot jam around the plates is a fun way to serve these. Serve with Vanilla Ice Cream.

Vanilla Ice Cream

4 egg yolks
½ cup sugar
2 cups cream, or 1 cup cream + 1 cup milk
2 teaspoons vanilla

Beat egg yolks with sugar until light and creamy. Heat cream. Add a little heated cream to egg mixture to warm, and then pour egg mixture into the cream. Heat until thickened, stirring all the time, being careful not to curdle the mixture. Remove from heat and transfer to another dish to cool. Place in ice cream machine or in a dish covered with plastic wrap in the freezer. Whisk every now and then until set. This will give the ice cream a smooth consistency.

Serves 8

I got the idea for this dessert from something similar I had in a restaurant in Jaffa, where I was meeting a former boyfriend for dinner. We had "gone together" when I was eleven years old and I hadn't seen him since. To be honest, he looked better at eleven than he did all these years later, and it certainly didn't help him any that this dessert was serious competition for my attention.

1 package phyllo pastry
melted butter for brushing phyllo
1 cup pressed or fresh dates, chopped
1 cup chopped pecans
1 cup chocolate chips

Preheat oven to 350F/180C. Brush one sheet of phyllo pastry with melted butter. Fold in half and brush with more butter. Cut in half and scatter dates, pecans and chocolate chips along one edge. Tuck in the sides and roll up into a cigar shape. Continue with the rest of the pastry. Brush the tops with more melted butter, sprinkle with Pecan Praline and bake for 15 minutes or until golden brown. The phyllo "cigars" may be frozen before baking. To serve, place a phyllo cigar on each plate and drizzle with Halva Sauce, or put sauce on plate first, with cigar on top.

Pecan Praline

1 cup sugar
½ cup water
1 cup pecans

Heat sugar and water in a heavy saucepan over high heat, until it caramelizes. Place pecans on a greased baking sheet. Pour the caramelized sugar over the pecans and allow to set. Break into pieces and grind in a food processor. Store in an airtight container in the freezer. It's delicious sprinkled over ice creams.

Halva Sauce

½ cup halva
1 cup cream

Crush halva with the back of a spoon. Mix it into the cream until smooth.

Phyllo with Halva Sauce

Passion-Filled Pavlova

To Assemble

Vanilla Ice Cream (recipe page 174)
Mars Bar Chocolate Sauce
strawberries

Peel paper from Pavlova and place on a serving platter. Fill with balls of Vanilla Ice Cream and drizzle with Mars Bar Chocolate Sauce. Scatter with strawberries – if made into Friandise (recipe page 183), all the better.

Mars Bar Chocolate Sauce

3-4 Mars bars or any caramel-filled chocolate
2 tablespoons butter
¼ cup milk

Heat butter, milk and Mars bars until melted. Allow to thicken, adding more milk if necessary.

Serves 8–10
This is the easiest dessert to make and an instant attention getter.

Pavlova

1 cup egg whites (approximately 8 eggs)
pinch of salt
2 cups sugar
1 teaspoon vinegar
1 teaspoon cornstarch

Beat egg whites with a pinch of salt for a few minutes. Before they get stiff, begin to add the sugar gradually. Add the vinegar and beat until stiff. Fold in cornstarch. Cover a baking sheet with a piece of greased foil or parchment paper. Smooth mixture over the foil to form a rectangle, making the sides slightly higher than the base. Preheat oven to 400F/200C, turn down to 250F/125C, and bake Pavlova for 20 minutes. Turn oven off and leave for another 20 minutes. Remove and allow to cool.

Ice Cream &
Hot Chocolate Sauce

Serves 8–10

This was one of the desserts I served at my second wedding. It's scrumptious and foolproof – unlike the made-to-flop husband I had chosen!

Crème Brûlé Custard

2 cups cream

2 tablespoons sugar

5 egg yolks

1 teaspoon cornstarch,
   mixed to a paste with a little cream

2 teaspoons vanilla extract

Heat cream. Whisk sugar with egg yolks. Add about a tablespoon of heated cream to eggs and then pour the egg mixture into the cream. Add vanilla and cornstarch paste. Heat, stirring, until thickened. Pour into serving dish. Cool, cover with plastic wrap and place in fridge to set and cool completely.

Almond Praline

1 cup sugar

½ cup water

1 cup skinned almonds

Melt sugar and water in a heavy saucepan over high heat until it caramelizes and turns a rich golden brown color. Place almonds on a greased baking sheet, and pour the caramelized sugar over the nuts. Allow to cool, break into pieces and grind in food processor.

Caramel Sauce

2 tablespoons brown sugar

1 cup cream

Heat sugar in heavy saucepan until it caramelizes. Add cream and stir until smooth. Set aside to cool.

Caramel Sauce

To Assemble

1 package phyllo pastry
½ cup butter, melted

Using one sheet of phyllo pastry at a time, brush with melted butter. Place another sheet of pastry on top and brush with more melted butter. Sprinkle with Almond Praline and slice into 2"/5cm squares. Continue doing so until you have 4 per person. Place on a greased baking sheet and bake in a preheated 350F/180C oven for about 10 minutes or until golden brown. Cool.

Spread a generous amount of Crème Brûlé Custard on a square of the prepared phyllo pastry. Place in center of plate. Repeat with another 2 pieces of prepared phyllo pastry, placing a fourth piece on top. Drizzle with Caramel Sauce and sprinkle with some extra Almond Praline.

Serves 6–8

These are seriously luxurious. To quote Frank Lloyd Wright, "Give me the luxuries of life and I will willingly do without the necessities."

Crème Brûlé

2 cups cream

2 tablespoons sugar

5 egg yolks

1–2 tablespoons Franjelico

1 cup toasted, chopped hazelnuts

Scald cream in a heavy saucepan. Beat together sugar and egg yolks until light and creamy. Add a quarter of this mixture to the heated cream, a spoonful at a time and then add the rest of it. Reduce heat and whisk until mixture thickens. Add Franjelico, stirring on heat for a few more minutes. Pour into individual ramekin dishes and allow to cool before placing in fridge to set. Sprinkle with toasted hazelnuts and top each ramekin with a Candy Cage. I serve these on a plate with strawberry Friandise on the side.

Candy Cages

1 cup sugar

½ cup water

In a heavy saucepan, heat sugar and water, but do not stir. Watch carefully when mixture starts to brown as it burns quickly. Gently tilt the pan to distribute the sugar as it caramelizes. When it reaches a rich golden color, remove from stove and allow to cool slightly so that it gets a little sticky.

Cover a soup ladle with tin foil. Dip a wooden spoon into the caramelized sugar and run the spoon in a crisscross fashion over the foil on the back of the soup ladle. Allow to set for a few minutes. Gently remove the foil from the ladle and allow "cage" to harden. Cover the spoon with more foil and repeat until all the caramelized sugar mixture has been used. When the candy cages have hardened on the foil, gently peel the foil away. Place a candy cage over each ramekin dish. If any of the candy cages breaks while peeling off the foil, "glue" it together with a little re-heated caramelized sugar mixture.

Friandise

These are the perfect ending to a meal. Men are knocked out when presented with them, & they are simple to make!

use any hard fruit such as strawberries, tangerines, grapes, or even nuts

1 cup sugar

½ cup water

In a heavy saucepan, heat the sugar and water together until the sugar caramelizes. Dip the pieces of fruit one at a time into the caramel and allow to harden on greased foil. In hot weather these should not be left too long before being eaten. Serve Friandise after dinner, as a dessert decoration or with a cheese board.

Candy Cages

Amorous Apple Tart & Cinnamon Ice Cream

Serves 8–10
Simply senasational and totally seductive!

5 Granny Smith apples, peeled and cored
4 tablespoons butter
2/3 cup sugar
1 package puff pastry
2–3 tablespoons additional sugar

Preheat oven to 400F/200C. Use an 11"/28cm frying pan that can go in the oven. Melt butter and sugar until it caramelizes. As the center starts getting light brown, gently move the mixture around until a light golden color emerges. Remove from heat.

Slice the apples into 10 slices per apple. Place in a circle on top of the caramelized sugar in the pan, making sure there are no gaps in between. You should have enough apples to make double rows.

Roll out the pastry enough to fit over the apples, trimming a little off the sides if necessary. Place the pastry over the apples, turning back the edges about ½"/2cm. If the dough is short on any of the sides, use the pieces that were trimmed and press them onto the dough to make up the shortfall. Prick with a fork, sprinkle with the additional sugar and bake for 25 minutes or until puffed and golden brown. Allow to cool. Place a serving plate over the cake in the pan and turn upside down, being careful not to spill any of the caramelized sugar. I cover my hand and part of my arm with a dishtowel to prevent any spillage from burning me.

If made ahead of time, re-heat on the stove, in the pan, until it bubbles around the edges and then invert as above. Serve with Cinnamon Ice Cream.

Cinnamon Ice Cream

3 egg yolks

½ cup sugar

2 cups cream (if a less rich
   ice cream is desired, use half-and-half,
   or 1 cup cream and 1 cup milk)

1 teaspoon vanilla extract

2 teaspoons cinnamon

Beat egg yolks and sugar together. Scald cream in a heavy saucepan and add egg mixture a few spoonfuls at a time at first and then add the rest. Add vanilla and cinnamon. Heat, stirring, until slightly thickened. Remove and allow to cool. Place in ice cream machine or in a 9"/23cm spring-form pan covered with plastic wrap. Place in freezer.

Bewitching Black

Meringue

5 egg whites
1 cup sugar
1 tablespoon cornstarch
1 tablespoon flour

Preheat oven to 250F/125C. Beat egg whites till very stiff. Gradually add sugar, beating the whole time. Fold in flour and cornstarch. Divide mixture in half and spread onto parchment baking paper forming two 9"/23cm circles. Bake for about 1 to 1½ hours. The Meringue will harden on cooling.

Filling

3 cups whipping cream
icing/powdered sugar to taste
1 jar or can strawberry pie filling*
fresh strawberries cut in half

Beat cream with sugar until it forms peaks. Place one layer of chocolate cake on a plate. Spread with a generous amount of whipped cream and strawberry pie filling. Scatter with fresh strawberries, making sure some stick out at the edges. Top with meringue layer and repeat procedure, reserving enough whipped cream for the top. The top layer must be a meringue.

*If not available use 2 x 16oz/450g packages frozen strawberries. Purée and sweeten with sugar to taste. Heat with 2 tablespoons cornstarch mixed to a paste with water. Allow to cool completely.

Serves 12
This looks spectacular and is so easy to put together.

Chocolate Cake

1 cup butter
1½ cups sugar
4 eggs
3 cups all-purpose flour
pinch of salt
3 teaspoons baking powder
2 tablespoons cocoa
1 cup of milk

Preheat oven to 350F/180C. Cream the butter and sugar. Add eggs and beat again. Add dry ingredients alternately with milk and beat well. Pour into a 9"/23cm cake pan and bake for 30 minutes or until a knife inserted into the middle comes out clean. Cool and turn onto a wire rack. When completely cooled, slice cake through the center into two equal rounds.

Forest Cake

To Serve

maraschino cherries
7oz/200g sweetened milk chocolate for baking
cocoa

Top with the rest of the whipped cream, dot with maraschino cherries and broken pieces of chocolate standing up
in the whipped cream. For chocolate pieces, melt 7oz/
200g chocolate. Spread on a piece of foil and allow to cool
and harden. Remove foil and break chocolate into pieces.
Sprinkle cocoa through a small sieve over the cake.

Out of This World

Cream Cheese Filling

> 4 x 8oz/250ml tubs cream cheese
>
> 1 cup sugar
>
> 4 eggs
>
> 2 teaspoons vanilla extract
>
> 8oz/250ml heavy or whipping cream
>
> 1 tablespoon flour

For my second wedding, I made three of these cheesecakes and placed them on three levels of a wedding cake stand. I decorated the sides by melting 2 x 7oz/200g slabs of sweetened milk chocolate and spreading it over greased foil. When it hardened, I broke off pieces, more or less the same height as the sides of the cake and stuck them onto the sides of the cake using icing. I then tied bunches of gold raffia around the chocolate, finishing with a knot in the front of the cake. The top was decorated with bunches of glazed fruit.

The desired richness of the cake will determine which cream cheese to use. Philadelphia is the richest.

Preheat oven to 350F/180C. Place cream cheese and sugar in the bowl of an electric mixer and beat well. Add eggs and beat again. Mix in the rest of the ingredients, adding the flour last. Pour onto the Biscuit Base. Slowly drizzle the Mars Bar Sauce onto the Cream Cheese Filling. Use the point of a knife to make figure-eight swirls in the cheese mixture. Bake for 45 minutes. Turn oven off, open the door and allow the cake to rest for a further 45 minutes. Remove, cool and refrigerate overnight.

Biscuit Base

> 3 packets graham crackers
>   (there are 6 packets per box)
>
> ¾ cup butter, melted

Crush the crackers in a food processor and mix with the melted butter. Place in a 10"/26cm springform pan and place in freezer while preparing the filling.

Mars Bar Sauce

> 1 tablespoon butter
>
> 1 large Mars bar, or any good quality caramel-filled chocolate bar
>
> 3–4 tablespoons milk

Melt butter in a saucepan. Add chocolate and 3 tablespoons milk and heat until chocolate has melted, adding more milk to obtain a smooth consistency. Set aside.

Mars Bar Chocolate Cheesecake

Pecan Praline Paradise Cheesecake

Prepare the Biscuit Base (recipe page 188) and Pecan Praline (recipe page 176)

Filling

4 x 8oz/250ml tubs cream cheese

1¼ cups brown sugar

4 eggs

3 teaspoons vanilla

2 tablespoons flour

1 cup chopped pecans

Preheat oven to 350F/180C. Beat together cream cheese and sugar with electric mixer. Add eggs and beat again. Add the vanilla and flour, mixing well. Fold in the nuts last. Pour Filling onto Biscuit Base and bake for 45 minutes or until the cake has set. Heat ingredients for Topping and gently pour over cake. Allow to cool and place in fridge overnight.

When ready to serve, scatter Pecan Praline over the top, pipe with whipped cream and decorate with whole pecans. Place a few of the Caramelized Sugar Sticks on the cake between the other toppings.

Topping

½ cup brown sugar

3 tablespoons butter

1 x 250 ml/8oz thick cream

Caramelized Sugar Sticks

1 cup sugar

½ cup water

Caramelize 1 cup sugar with ½ cup water. Allow to cool slightly and drizzle onto foil, forming odd-shaped, long stringy sticks. Allow to harden. Peel foil away gently. Use to garnish desserts as well as cakes.

I can smugly say that I have yet to taste a better cheesecake than mine.
My obsession with making the perfect cheesecake started when I lived in L.A. near the Cheese Cake Factory. I was amazed that there could be so many fabulous combinations. When I returned to South Africa, I was determined to come up with my own formula that would not only be as good as theirs, but beat them. And I did! Oh, and one other thing – if it's a proposal you're after, these never fail.

Wicked White

One of my closest friends was in prison for stock exchange irregularities. Out on a doctor's visit, he called to say that he could come and have tea with me on his way back to jail. Since he loved my cheesecakes, I had one waiting for him. We drank tea and ate cheesecake under the watchful eye of his guard. Telling the guard that he wanted to talk to me privately, we were allowed to go into my bedroom. Once there, he pulled me towards him and started to kiss me, tearing off his clothes and trying to get mine off as well! I was so shocked I told him he must get dressed and go back to jail. I didn't see the funny side then, but I laugh about it now and am convinced it was the cheesecake!

Prepare the Biscuit Base (recipe page 188)

4 x 8oz/250ml tubs cream cheese

1 cup sugar

4 eggs

1 tablespoon lemon juice

8oz/250ml whipping cream

2 tablespoons flour

3 teaspoons vanilla

2 x 7oz/200g slabs white chocolate chopped coarsely in food processor

Friandise (recipe page 183)

Preheat oven to 350F/180C. Beat the cream cheese and sugar in an electric mixer. Add eggs and beat again. Add lemon juice, cream, flour and vanilla and beat again. Fold in half the white chocolate. Pour cheese mixture onto Biscuit Base and bake for 45 minutes. Turn oven off & open the door. Leave the cake in the open oven for a further 45 minutes. Cool and place in fridge to set overnight.

Melt the rest of the white chocolate over hot water or in the microwave. Coat a piece of plastic bubble wrap with it. Allow to harden in fridge. Peel off the plastic and break the chocolate into fairly long pieces. Decorate cake with the chocolate pieces and Friandise.

Chocolate Cheesecake

Index

Acknowledgements

My overwhelming gratitude goes to my two sons Mathew and Jamie. Not only were they my prime tasters with their exquisite palates, they were also my greatest inspiration and my most compelling motivators. They are the finest examples of who I want to be when I grow up.

I have no idea how to express my gratitude towards my mother, Molly, and sister, Louise. However much I enthuse or heap praise, it will still not come close to what they mean to me. During the birth of this book, their patience was endless, their contribution enormous and their presence was "chicken soup for my soul." Louise is the reason this book is published.

This is not *just* a recipe book – this is a creation that was born from a huge amount of anxiety, trauma, pain and suffering. It was their love and my children's that got me through, pulled me along and carried me over to the side of freedom, happiness and laughter.

I am more than grateful to my publisher, Elena Mazour, who unhesitatingly took on this project. There aren't enough words to thank her for giving me this opportunity of a lifetime. And then she brought in the most astonishing editor, Penny Hozy, the creative design genius, Robert López, and the terrific photographer, Gregory Talas. None of them ever lost their cool when I more than once lost mine.

On my journey of food and men, I met the most mouth-watering ingredient of all in the form of Gene Taubman. His passion for cooking challenged me to new culinary heights but more than that, he showed me how decent, honorable and noble a man can be.

I am also eternally grateful to the St. Francis Al-Anon group who taught me to accept with serenity the things I cannot change, to have the courage to change the things I can, and the wisdom to know the difference.

Philippa